PRAISE FOR

THE ALWAYS GOD

"In our ever-changing world, there is one constant: God never leaves, never forgets, and never changes. Let Jarrett Stephens direct to you toward truths that will ground you in God's love and show you how to let his grace turn your season around. I highly recommend *The Always God*!"

—DARRYL STRAWBERRY,
four-time World Series champion and evangelist

"In these pages, you'll find empathy, wisdom, encouragement, and a thoroughly biblical perspective for times when God seems distant or disinterested. Jarrett Stephens doesn't flinch as he courageously confronts some of the most nettlesome issues that vex so many followers of Jesus. Whatever you do, don't miss this journey toward wholeness. Let Jarrett lead you to a place of genuine hope and faith!"

—LEE STROBEL, bestselling author
of *The Case for Christ* and *The Case for Miracles*

"Do you wonder if God has forgotten you? Are your circumstances and situations getting the best of you? Psalm 90:2 says, 'From everlasting to everlasting you are God.' But sometimes we don't realize it and don't live it. In *The Always God,* Jarrett Stephens shows us that the biblical God who sees, hears, and speaks is our same God today. If you are broken, fearful, angry, anxious, or lost, the always God is always here for you."

—KYLE IDLEMAN, senior pastor of Southeast Christian Church
and author of *Not a Fan* and *Don't Give Up*

"Jarrett Stephens is a man who knows and loves God—who is always present, who is forever faithful, and who never stops working in our lives. *The Always God* is filled with insights, encouragement, and promises from God's Word that will fill you with faith, hope, and love for the One who never fails. Read this book and deepen your confidence in the grace and glory of our God."

—JACK GRAHAM, pastor of Prestonwood Baptist Church and leader of PowerPoint Ministries

"We read about God's promises for love and protection, but what do we do when it feels like he's breaking them? Jarrett Stephens eloquently guides us to see God as the same God of fulfilled promises—yesterday, today, and forever. *The Always God* shows us how to live in faith and walk through all that is in front of us by remembering who our God truly is."

—LEVI LUSKO, lead pastor of Fresh Life Church and bestselling author

"*The Always God* is a refreshing, comforting reminder of the good news that God is for us. If you, like me, sometimes struggle to feel the closeness of God or sometimes wonder whether he hears you or is on your side, read this book carefully. You will find the strong hope of Jesus in its pages."

—JARED C. WILSON, assistant professor of pastoral ministry at Spurgeon College, author in residence at Midwestern Seminary, and author of *The Imperfect Disciple*

"*The Always God* is a tour de force through the labyrinth of questions surrounding human suffering. The main path is well worn: 'If God is both good and all powerful, why doesn't he do something to eliminate, or at least alleviate, suffering?' Jarrett Stephens guides us through the maze with bracing biblical truth and pastoral compassion. This is a therapeutic theology."

—MARK E. MOORE, PHD, author of *Core 52*

"In this book, Jarrett Stephens opens a window into our souls as he unveils the honest questions we ask about God's presence in our pivotal moments. His clear language and profound yet practical answers compel us to discover the always God in a superior dimension and leave us with a deep thirst for his constant presence."

—RAMON MEDINA, Spanish global pastor
at Champion Forest Baptist Church

"Everyone struggles to find and understand God in this often upside-down world. With a pastor's heart, Jarrett weaves solid theology with relatable stories to guide us in this journey. Read this book for hope and understanding, but don't be surprised to see your faith grow stronger."

—MARK LANIER, trial lawyer
and author of *Christianity On Trial*

"*The Always God* is a timely, much-needed reminder of the steady attributes of God. Whether you're struggling with faith, looking to grow in your walk with Jesus, or just needing a fresh reminder of our always God, this book will meet you where you are. My good friend Jarrett Stephens reminds us of an ever-present God, who sees us, hears us, and speaks to us in the midst of every circumstance. Read this book—and be ready to meet the always God there."

—SHANE PRUITT, national next-gen director
for the North American Mission Board (NAMB)
and author of *9 Common Lies Christians Believe*

"Trying to comprehend a supernatural God can be so difficult. We can't see, hear, or touch God, which makes us doubt his existence. But Jarrett Stephens has given us a remarkable gift with his new book, *The Always God*. More than a gift, it's a key—a powerful tool for unlocking a sense of God's presence in our lives. In your dark moments, when you feel that God isn't there or has abandoned you, reach for this book."

—PHIL COOKE, PHD, media producer
and author of *Maximize Your Influence*

"In *The Always God,* Jarrett presents helpful handholds as he moves us through the questions we all ask at some point in our faith journey. His book is engaging, practical, reflective, and will make you love the Lord more. I am always looking for resources to stir my affections for Jesus, and this is one of them."

—JONATHAN POKLUDA, lead pastor
of Harris Creek Baptist Church and author of *Outdated*

"*The Always God* is a timely, powerful word for our world, where nothing good seems to last. We need to know God will always be with us and for us. Be encouraged by this message of the timeless love of God."

—GREGG MATTE, pastor of Houston's First Baptist Church
and author of *Difference Makers*

THE
ALWAYS
GOD

THE
ALWAYS
GOD

HE HASN'T CHANGED AND
YOU ARE NOT FORGOTTEN

JARRETT
STEPHENS

Foreword by Sheila Walsh

MULTNOMAH

To my mom and dad, Glynn and Cheryl Stephens,
thank you for your love, encouragement, and support.
I am proud to be your son.

From everlasting to everlasting you are God.

PSALM 90:2

The word *always* is interesting. It gets its meaning from what we attach it to. It can bear great news, such as "The food is always amazing here!" It can also let us know to lower our expectations, such as "The service is always slow here." When attached to faith in God, however, it can raise as many questions as it answers. You may have faced some of these:

I believe that God is always present, so why do I feel all alone?
I believe that God is always working for my good, so why didn't I get that job?
I believe that God always answers prayer, so why does heaven seem silent?

These kinds of questions can shake our faith to the core.

I remember being challenged once by a woman with heart-breaking questions of her own. It was several years ago. I was speaking at a conference in South Africa, and she had waited until the crowd was gone before she approached me. She was angry, but I could tell that just beneath that mask, she was hurting. She told me I had said two things on the platform that couldn't possibly *both* be true. I would have to pick one. I asked her what they were.

She replied, "You said that God is loving and God is powerful."

I told her I believe that both of those things are true. She asked me to explain the death of her child and then collapsed into my arms in tears.

What she was facing is one of the greatest challenges to faith. If God is loving and powerful, why would he allow any of the tragedies that strike our lives? When prayer seems to go no higher than the bedroom ceiling or when one more door is slammed on us, it's tempting to believe that God has forgotten where we live or doesn't care about what's happening to us.

In uncertain times, *The Always God* is a must-read for all of us. I have had the privilege of sitting under the teaching ministry of Jarrett Stephens for years. It's a joy to call him my friend. One of his greatest gifts is his ability to combine transparency and truth. He is honest and vulnerable about his own life and the questions he's dealt with. He's not afraid to ask the difficult questions, but he always leads us back to the powerful promises in God's Word. You won't want to rush through this book. It will make you think and challenge you to be honest with yourself and with God. If you've been struggling in your faith or simply want to grow stronger, then you have the perfect guidebook in your hands. When you turn the final page, you'll have a fresh confidence in these foundational truths:

God is always here.
God is always working.
God is always faithful.

Always.

—*Sheila Walsh*

CONTENTS

~~~~~~~~

INTRODUCTION

~~~~~~

Always? Are you sure?

God is always *for* you. He is always a supernatural God, who will do miracles for you as he has done in the past.

God is always *with* you. He is always watching, always caring, and always reaching.

God is always *in* you. He is always providing unlimited power and encouragement.

And all God's people said, "Are you sure?"

Let me assure you, I *am* sure. Except when I'm not.

Never waver, never doubt, never question—as a pastor, I feel like this is the posture of certainty I'm supposed to take in every situation. I should always have the answers, right? When I don't? I should be confident and act like I do! But if I'm being honest, I am not always certain what God is up to and find myself confused by what he's allowing in my life. (Can I lose my pastor's license for just *writing* that last sentence?)

It's uncomfortable for me to admit, but I relate well to the father who had a sick child and told Jesus, "I believe; help my unbelief!" (Mark 9:24, ESV). My experiences in life bear out this complexity. When I read God's Word or hear other pastors preach from it, I always want to respond with "Amen!" But then life throws a curveball, and my "Amen!" turns to "Are you sure?"

I do believe God is good all the time and all the time God is good. "Amen!"

But when I was being sexually abused by my Little League coach from age eight to twelve, I struggled to believe this truth about God. "Are you sure?" ambushed my "Amen!"

I do believe every perfect gift comes down from the Father. "Amen!"

But when my wife had a miscarriage, I struggled to believe this was true in my case. "Are you sure?" ambushed my "Amen!"

I do believe God is always seeking the lost, pursuing the one who is far from him. "Amen!"

But when my brother walked away from his faith and rebuffed my attempts to share Jesus with him, I struggled with some serious doubt. "Are you sure?" ambushed my "Amen!"

I do believe God is always with us, taking care of his own. "Amen!"

But when Mike, my friend and mentor who's one of the most faithful Christians I knew, was diagnosed with cancer and died, I struggled to believe God was coming through on what he'd promised. "Are you sure?" ambushed my "Amen!"

I want to believe I'm the only one with these struggles, but I know I'm not. I've been a pastor now for more than twenty years. I get to be with people in their best moments—"Life is awesome! Let's take a celebration selfie!"—the birth of children, beautiful weddings, picking up finally sober loved ones from rehab. And I get to be with people in their heart-crushing moments—"Why is this happening?"—the death of a baby, an unexpected divorce, dropping no-longer-sober loved ones back off at rehab.

I bet you've been there. Something awful happened, disrupting your life and disorienting your faith. Your life had been comfortable and you were confident. Suddenly your life was chaotic and you were confused. Doubts crept in where there had always been certainty. It wasn't that you lost your faith, because you still believed, but your faith was now challenged by questions that had never occurred to you or bothered you before.

For you, it might be . . .

Someone you loved got a cancer diagnosis and then quickly he was gone.

You've been desperately searching for a job, but no doors seem to be opening.

You discover a text exchange between your spouse and a stranger. You read the words over and over, trying to understand, but deep down you already know. It feels like a bomb is settling in your stomach.

You raised your child to love Jesus, but you are realizing she just doesn't love him. Your heart breaks with every step she takes away from God.

You don't know what to do. But you do believe that God is the only one who can help you. You have prayed prayers on top of prayers, but God has been strangely quiet, and it leaves you wrestling with the disquieting question of whether he even hears you.

You've been there, right? We've *all* gone through circumstances that cause us to question what God is doing. We ask, *Is he aware of what's happening? Does he even care?*

We read in the Bible about miracles God performed and wonder if maybe God coming through for people like that is relegated to the past. God did that back then, but life seems to prove he doesn't work in the same way now. We read promises God made, like "Never will I leave you; never will I forsake you" (Hebrews 13:5), and we don't want to admit that it just doesn't feel that way at times.

Have you ever wondered if maybe God has forgotten you? If we are going to be completely honest—and that's exactly what I hope we'll be, so let's agree to be totally honest with each other throughout this book—I bet you have felt pretty sure that God has forgotten you. When you considered the confusing circumstances of your life and the long list of unanswered desperate voice mails you've left God, this conclusion is painful but seems unavoidable.

I realize you may not be comfortable being this honest—it

might be more real and raw than you typically permit yourself to be—but it may help you to know that you're not alone.

In fact, *Jesus* has been there. On the night before he was crucified, he went to a garden where "he sank into a pit of suffocating darkness" (Mark 14:33, MSG). He was real and raw, saying, "My soul is overwhelmed with sorrow to the point of death" (Matthew 26:38). We see Jesus questioning God's plan for him. The next day he cries out, wondering if God had forsaken him.

But I have good news: you are not alone.

More good news: you can go from "Are you sure?" back to "Amen!"

Jesus did.

I have too.

If you're struggling with a little doubt, I believe you need two things.

First, you need to be reassured that God is still God—that he is *always* God. You need to be reassured that you can stand firm in your faith, fully trusting him, knowing that he will carry you and not drop you and that your trust in him will not be in vain.

Second, you need to be invited to push through your questions to a deeper faith. Peter tells us that we go through the painful fire of these trials so that our faith can be tested, proved, and refined (1 Peter 1:6–9), which will lead us into "an inexpressible and glorious joy" (verse 8). I've noticed that just about all the heroes in the Bible—as well as the people I personally know whose spiritual maturity I admire and long to emulate—had their faith galvanized through a crucible of unwanted trials and uncomfortable doubts. If we walk that same path, we can end up spiritually mature with a deeper faith, just as the heroes of the Bible also grew.

I wrote this book for you because I've been where you are. As a pastor, I walk with people who are where you are: in the midst of a trial, needing to be reminded that our God is *always* God and needing to be invited to journey with him to a place of greater assurance and intimacy. Regardless of how things may seem, he is always the same and can always be trusted.

One time, after I spoke at a conference in Europe, my wife and I traveled to Prague. The city is amazing. It has so much character and history. It was the vacation of a lifetime! And it was just the two of us—we left our four daughters at home with their grandparents. (I haven't mentioned yet—I have *four* daughters and a wife. I am the president of my own sorority. I do have a male dog, but he's fixed, so he doesn't really count.)

At first, we were just in awe of Prague. The city is beautiful, ancient, and mysterious. But we quickly realized that we were disoriented. We loved being there, but we weren't sure where to go or what to do. Fortunately, we had booked a bike tour. An *electric* bike tour, that is—I didn't want to have to work too hard because I was on vacation! We were newbies, but the tour guide was familiar with Prague and navigated us through the city. By the end of the tour, the city felt familiar, and we spent the rest of our time in Prague with confidence.

I think many, at first, are just in awe of God. God and his Word are beautiful, ancient, and mysterious. But then when adversity assaults us, we can become disoriented. We still love God, but we aren't sure exactly where to go or what to do. In those moments, we need a tour guide—someone who is familiar with suffering and someone who can help us navigate through our doubts and questions until our faith feels more familiar again and we can walk with confidence.

I would love to be that tour guide for you. That's the heart behind this book. If you let me, here's where I want to take you.

TOUR ONE: ALWAYS HERE

We all face situations that cause us to wonder whether God really knows or cares about what we are up against. In this section, we will seek to answer questions so many of us have asked:

Does God really see me and the situation I'm going through? If so, why does it feel like he doesn't? Is he ignoring me?

Does God really hear me? I know that he claims to listen, but if so, how do you explain all my unanswered prayers?

Does God really speak to me? Yeah, I can read the Bible, but I need God to help me with the decision I have to make and to guide me through the problem I'm having. I'm listening, so if he's speaking, I don't get it.

TOUR TWO: ALWAYS WORKING

Maybe God is always here, but is he doing anything?

If you've asked that question, I get it. I've been there. And as a pastor, I have met with thousands of people over the years, and most are honest and share their struggles with me. I've noticed some themes, and I want to walk with you through some questions I have wondered and have heard over and over:

Why isn't God pursuing this person I love who is far from him? I thought God wants everyone to be saved!

Can God truly restore my life? Sometimes I think I'm just too broken. Maybe even God can't heal me.

I worry all the time, and I really need God to calm my anxiety. How do I get the peace that he promises?

God tells us not to fear, but I am afraid about so many things. It doesn't help to tell me not to fear; I already know I shouldn't. I can't seem to stop. Why won't God take away my fear?

I feel so alone. If God is with me, I just can't feel it. Can he do something about my loneliness?

It's probably a sin, but I get angry—a lot. And the problem seems to actually be getting worse! How can God help me with my anger?

I feel so guilty about something I've done. Does God really forgive my sin? If he does, why don't I feel forgiven?

TOUR THREE: ALWAYS FAITHFUL

God asks us to put our faith in him. In fact, he tells us that it's impossible to please him without faith. This sounds great; we all like the idea of faith. But I've found that it doesn't always come easily. People in churches around the country have told me about their struggles with faith. They whisper questions like these:

> *Can I really trust God? If I do, what if he doesn't come through for me?*
> *I want to put my hope in God, but what if he disappoints me?*

Can you have an unwavering confidence that God is always here and always working? Can you get to a place where, no matter what happens, your "Amen!" overwhelms your "Are you sure?"

It's been a wild and sometimes painful journey, but that's where God has taken me and where I believe he will take you as you read this book. My prayer is that you will discover in a very personal and powerful way just how faithful the always God really is.

So, are you ready? Let's go.

ALWAYS HERE

CHAPTER 1

ALWAYS SEEING

~~~~~~~~

*Does God really see me? If so, why does it feel
like he doesn't? Is he ignoring me?*

'll never forget the phone call. My sister and her family were
visiting us, and we were on our way to eat lunch. As we drove
to the restaurant, I got a phone call from one of my college
roommates from back in the day. I normally would have picked
up, but because my sister was in town and we were catching up, I
decided to let the call go to voice mail. About ten minutes passed.
We were all piling out of the car to head into the restaurant when
the phone rang again. It was the same friend.

I've been in ministry long enough to know that back-to-back
phone calls in a short time span are rarely good. I told my family
to go in, and I took the phone call.

"Did you hear about Zac?"

No greeting. No pleasantries. Just this question.

Zac, another roommate from college, was one of the funniest
people I have ever met. A good comparison is Chandler from
Friends. Sarcastic. Witty. Quick with a comeback. Everyone who
knew Zac liked him.

When we graduated college, I moved to Dallas and he went
back home to northwest Arkansas. We didn't remain in close
contact through the years. We would send texts back and forth
every now and then. We followed each other on social media,
and occasionally he'd make fun of me in a comment.

Zac had married a few years ago and then had a son. He and his wife, Kelly, were very open on social media about their journey raising their son, Everett (or Ev), who was diagnosed with achondroplasia shortly after his birth. Most people know it as dwarfism. Because of his son's condition, Zac had been on my mind a lot and I prayed for him often.

Zac and Kelly were doing an amazing job at not only raising Ev but also helping to educate many people on the facts about dwarfism. They were living out their faith in a way that was honest, real, and transparent. I knew Zac was a believer, and I could tell caring for his son was taking him deeper in his walk with the Lord.

The day I got the phone call was Zac's forty-first birthday. Evidently, he left his house after having breakfast with Kelly and Ev and hopped on his brand-new motorcycle. As he was pulling out of the neighborhood, the bike got away from him and he ran into oncoming traffic. He died instantly.

Forty-one years old.

On his birthday.

Leaving behind a beautiful wife and three-year-old boy.

I felt numb. When I got off the phone and walked into the restaurant to join my family, my wife and sister immediately knew something was wrong. I told them the news and made it through lunch the best I could.

But I could not stop thinking about Zac. More than that, I could not get Kelly and Everett off my mind. None of it made sense to me.

How could this happen? What was God doing?

EYES LIKE ROZ

One of my girls' favorite movies when they were little was *Monsters, Inc.* Well, I'll be honest, this was one of *my* favorites. Who couldn't like the lead characters—er, monsters—James P. Sullivan and Mike Wazowski?

These two monsters were the exact opposite in personality but made a great team. Mike was the more responsible of the two but could be a bit of an airhead. Sulley was the larger-than-life, charismatic scare champion. Mike and Sulley partnered together at Monsters, Inc., to make sure the screams of boys and girls from all over the world kept their city powered.

They were supposed to file paperwork each day with Roz, a miserable and grumpy sluglike figure who had no love for Mike, his forgetfulness, or his schmoozing.

She constantly reminded him, "I'm watching you, Wazowski. Always watching."[1]

We don't find out until the end of the movie that Roz actually worked undercover for the Child Detection Agency (CDA) and knew exactly what Mike and Sulley had been up to the entire time—because she was "always watching."

I thought about Roz when writing this chapter because sometimes I wonder if Roz was better at watching Mike Wazowski than God is at watching us.

That's how I felt when I heard about Zac, especially when I thought about Kelly and Ev in the days following the accident.

Didn't God see that Kelly needed Zac? Didn't he see that Ev needed his dad? Why wasn't God watching?

Surely, you have felt that way before. Something happened and you felt as though God must be taking a nap or, worse, turning his back on you. Either way, he must not see what's going on. If he did, whatever was happening wouldn't be taking place.

It might have been . . .

A relationship that went wrong.

Someone else getting the promotion you deserved.

The story in the news about another innocent person being killed.

The way your kid is struggling.

The prayer you've prayed and prayed without an answer.

Zac's death led me on a journey to see what the Bible had to say about all this. I knew Scripture promised that God was aware of our lives and was present in the midst of difficulty, but I needed more clarity.

I had attended a four-year Bible school, gotten my master's at a seminary, and completed my doctoral studies.

I had read all about God's omniscience—that he knows everything.

I had written papers on his omnipotence—that he can do anything.

In classes, we had debated his immutability—that he never changes.

I *knew* intellectually what the Bible says about the nature and character of God, but I was having a really hard time *believing* it after Zac's death.

ANTHROPOMORPHIWHAA?

I have a little joke I sometimes share with people about myself: My family is from Mississippi. I grew up in Louisiana and went to college in Arkansas. That means I am never the smartest person in the room—*ever.* I certainly felt that way when I was introduced to the term *anthropomorphism.* I had never heard it before and couldn't pronounce it. You should have seen how many times I tried spelling it while writing this paragraph.

Let me save you some google time. *Anthropomorphism* is a big, fancy term that theologians use for ascribing human characteristics to God. In this section, we're going to explore why it's so important that . . .

God sees.

God hears.

God speaks.

Anthropomorphism ascribes to God the same physical functions we humans have so that we can better understand him and how he operates. For example, we might say,

> When God sees, he sees with his eyes.
> When God hears, he hears with his ears.
> When God speaks, he speaks with his mouth.

God does not physically have these functions of the human body because "God is spirit" (John 4:24). Anthropomorphism simply makes it a bit easier for us to fathom God.

As I dove into Scripture to understand what happened with Zac, it became abundantly obvious that although God may not have physical eyes, he sees farther, clearer, and more than we ever could.

For example, the Bible teaches over and over that God sees *what we do*. Listen to how the psalmist wrote it:

> From heaven the LORD looks down
>   and sees all mankind;
> from his dwelling place he watches
>   all who live on earth—
> he who forms the hearts of all,
>   who considers everything they do. (Psalm 33:13–15)

Did you notice that *all* was used three times in this passage? Read it again slowly. God sees everything. He "watches all" our deeds. Like for an all-star catcher in the major leagues, nothing gets past him—*nothing*. He sees everything we do.

God is sitting on his throne (more anthropomorphistic language), and from there, his eyes are on us no matter where we go.

> The eyes of the LORD are everywhere,
>   keeping watch on the wicked and the good. (Proverbs 15:3)

In Ezekiel 1:18, God is represented by an item that is "covered with eyes" (NLT). The implication is clear: God is a God who sees.

Jesus also taught that God the Father sees what we are doing. He sees when we pray. He sees when we give. In maybe Jesus's most famous teaching, the Sermon on the Mount, he shared that God sees even what we do in secret—when we give or pray without anyone else knowing, God knows (Matthew 6:6).

THERE'S AN APP FOR THAT

There seems to be an app for everything these days. Sometimes one comes along that catches the country's attention for a few weeks. Not too long ago, the craze was an app that aged your face. When people put their photographs in, this app automatically aged them, wrinkles and all, twenty, thirty, or forty years down the road. I tried it, and let me just say that my wife has *much* to look forward to!

I think people loved that app and shared their aging pictures not just because it was funny but because they wonder about their future. We question what we're going to look like. *Will my mind be as sharp? Will my body be strong and agile?*

While anthropomorphism has its strengths, one place it falls short is that when ascribing human characteristics to God, we also attach human weakness and frailty to him. I fear, like with FaceApp, we may assume God is aging, so to speak.

He's old.

He can't see as clearly as he once did. Getting a bit senile. Forgetful.

We might even think he has to take a nap from time to time. After all, that is what old people do. And if God is sleeping, he's not watching.

No wonder he's not seeing me in this tight spot I'm in. No wonder he's not coming through for me. He's sleeping.

Or is he?

We need to remember that although we use human traits to describe God, he is *not* human. In fact, the psalmist recorded that God never sleeps:

> I lift up my eyes to the mountains—
> > where does my help come from?
> My help comes from the LORD,
> > the Maker of heaven and earth.
>
> He will not let your foot slip—
> > he who *watches* over you will not slumber;
> indeed, he who *watches* over Israel
> > will neither slumber nor sleep.
>
> The LORD *watches* over you—
> > the LORD is your shade at your right hand;
> the sun will not harm you by day,
> > nor the moon by night.
>
> The LORD will keep you from all harm—
> > he will *watch* over your life;
> the LORD will *watch* over your coming and going
> > both now and forevermore. (Psalm 121, emphasis added)

How different God is from us! He doesn't sleep. He never needs a nap. We can know with confidence that nothing gets by him. He sees *everything* we do.

And because he is God, because he never sleeps, he also sees *what we don't.*

Remember where God is positioned? He is sitting on his throne, looking down from above.

GOD, THE COACH

I love football. My dream as I was growing up was to play college football, and I would have if any college coach had asked me! If I weren't a pastor, I promise you I'd be on the sidelines coaching football. Or maybe I'd be in the press box.

The press box is where most offensive and defensive coordinators spend their time during games. They sit there because of the perspective it offers. A coach on the sidelines can't see the whole field.

From the press box, the coordinators can see how the other team is lining up. They can watch which players are being substituted in and out. Because they see things from a different perspective, they can help determine a better strategy for winning the game. Where they are positioned in the press box allows them to see what others can't.

You get the analogy, right? Because of God's unique position, he sees things we don't. He doesn't see just our obedience and disobedience. He sees our motives—he sees *why* we obey or disobey.

I the LORD search the heart and examine the mind. (Jeremiah 17:10)

A person may think their own ways are right,
    but the LORD weighs the heart. (Proverbs 21:2)

Do you remember Samuel, the Old Testament prophet? God told him to visit a man named Jesse and to anoint one of Jesse's sons as the next king of Israel.

The first son's name was Eliab. Samuel was impressed with Eliab from the start.

He was strong.

He was tall.

He was handsome.

He was like Chris Hemsworth from the Marvel *Avengers* films. Who wouldn't want this Thor-like guy leading Israel? He was the first player chosen in all the pickup games. He dated any girl he was interested in because they all were interested in him. Surely, this was the next king.

But God was not nearly as impressed with Eliab.

> The LORD said to Samuel, "Do not consider his appearance or his height, for I have rejected him. The LORD does not look at the things people look at. People look at the outward appearance, but the LORD looks at the heart." (1 Samuel 16:7)

God sees what we don't! That is a good thing. Sometimes we think that he's not watching and that he doesn't see what we see. *Maybe he just doesn't care.* But I'm learning that it's what he sees and we *don't* that can be the biggest factor of all, the greatest proof that he cares more than we can imagine.

This is what the esteemed theologian Garth Brooks, in his song "Unanswered Prayers," tried to get across: "Some of God's greatest gifts are unanswered prayers."[2] God doesn't always respond to our prayers the way we want because he sees what we don't.

God is the ultimate air-traffic controller! According to *Travel + Leisure,* "aviation data companies like FlightAware keep track of all (or at least most) of the aircraft in our skies." According to their stats, in 2017 "there were an average of 9,728 planes—carrying 1,270,406 people—in the sky at any given time."[3]

God sees them all.

God keeps track of them all.

God makes the call to keep them from hitting one another in the sky and guides them to land safely.

In our lives, God sees *all* the pieces at play.

When it comes to our lives, he sees what will bring us harm.

He sees what will bring him the most glory.

He sees the effect of every choice we make before we make it!

This is why we can believe with confidence the promise Paul wrote to the church in Rome: "We know that in all things God works for the good of those who love him, who have been called according to his purpose" (Romans 8:28).

What we see is limited; what God sees is not. Theologian John Piper tweeted this statement, and I kept it as a favorite: "God is always doing 10,000 things in your life, and you may be aware of three of them."[4]

God sees what we don't! God sees the invisible reality of the spiritual battle taking place all around us right now. He even sees our adversary, the devil, prowling around like a roaring lion seeking to devour us (1 Peter 5:8). Paul wrote to the church in Ephesus,

> Put on the full armor of God, so that you can take your stand against the devil's schemes. For our struggle is not against flesh and blood, but against the rulers, against the authorities, against the powers of this dark world and against the spiritual forces of evil in the heavenly realms. (Ephesians 6:11–12)

If the curtains could be pulled back for us to see what God sees, we would be stunned. We would also be terrified. Because he loves and cares for us, God lets us know in his Word what is really going on, including the unseen battle we are in and the invisible enemies we are up against.

God sees what we do.

God sees what we don't.

God also sees *what has us down.*

THE GOD WHO SEES ME

I have always loved studying the different names of God. Throughout the Old Testament, God revealed himself and his ways to people by using different names.

In my first book, *The Mountains Are Calling,* I described Abraham's journey to Mount Moriah to obey God's command to sacrifice his son Isaac. I still can't imagine what was going through Abraham's mind as he made the three-day trek up the mountain.

After arriving at the specific place where he was to sacrifice his son, Abraham tied Isaac to the altar and raised his knife. In that moment of Abraham's complete surrender and obedience, God stopped him from going through with this sacrifice and instead provided a ram caught in a thicket. It was a substitute for Isaac. The Bible tells us, "Abraham called that place The Lord Will Provide. And to this day it is said, 'On the mountain of the Lord it will be provided'" (Genesis 22:14).

From that day on, God would be known as Jehovah-Jireh, which means "the Lord will provide." The names of God are revealed throughout Scripture, and I have found them to be extremely meaningful in my personal walk with him.

One of the names used to describe God's character and nature is El Roi. Can you guess what it means? "The God who sees."

How incredible is that? God is not just a God who sees. He is a personal God who sees *me.* He sees *you.*

I love that! And I love the following story of how this name of God was first revealed.

Abraham had a lot going for him in Scripture. He was wealthy. He was blessed by God. He was chosen to be the father of a nation that God promised to favor.

There was one issue, though. For Abraham to father a nation, he had to first father a child. But he and his wife, Sarah, could not get pregnant. I can only imagine the hurt and frustration that caused.

As a pastor, I have performed many baby dedications in worship services at our church. They are always times of celebration and happiness. The parents are over-the-top excited to show their newborn babies off to the congregation and also extremely nervous that a public spit-up or tantrum might occur. The grandparent paparazzi, as I refer to them, are in the front rows taking pictures.

It's a special day as parents dedicate the children God has given them and promise in front of the church to raise those children in a way that honors the Lord.

But it's a sad day, too, because while we are celebrating babies being born and new families being formed, it's a reminder to some people of what they *don't* have. God has yet to bless them with a child. They want to start a family, but God hasn't allowed it yet for some reason.

It's painful.

It's frustrating.

It's sad.

I've counseled plenty of couples facing this struggle, and it can cause strain in the relationship. It can also cause bitterness toward God if they're not careful.

When I read Abraham and Sarah's story, this is where I think they were. God had promised them a child, but he was not delivering. Every day that went by was another day of disappointment and a dream unfulfilled.

Finally, they got tired of waiting. God wasn't coming through on their timetable. He must have forgotten them or gone back on his promise. They decided to take the situation into their own hands.

God doesn't see their pain.

He must not be watching over them like he promised.

We'll just do what we need to do, they thought.

Sarah went to Abraham and said, "The Lord has kept me

from having children. Go, sleep with my slave; perhaps I can build a family through her" (16:2).

Problem solved, right? Hardly. Instead, it was problem *started*. This is usually how it works when we take things into our own hands.

Things went bad almost as soon as Hagar learned she was pregnant. Sarah became jealous and bitter toward Hagar. The Bible says she "dealt harshly" with Hagar (verse 6, ESV).

Hagar was just a servant. She had no real rights. She was simply doing what her master told her to do. Now she was in trouble, even despised, for it.

She had no one to plead her case to.

She had no one to turn to.

She had nowhere to go.

So, she ran away.

Hagar ran into the desert to get away from Sarah and from her situation. She had been treated unjustly and was a broken woman.

She was tired.

She was alone.

I can't imagine the pain she was in. I can't imagine the sense of hopelessness, the heartache, the grief. I bet she thought that no one cared and that God had forgotten her.

It was in this moment of brokenness and despair that an angel of the Lord appeared to her and told her to go back and submit to Abraham and Sarah. The angel promised that Hagar would have a son and that he would have offspring too numerous to count.

God revealed himself to her. Listen to her response: "She gave this name to the LORD who spoke to her: 'You are the God who sees me,' for she said, 'I have now seen the One who sees me'" (verse 13).

In that moment, Hagar gave God a new name. I've never

thought of naming God. It seems above my pay grade. But Hagar used this amazing moment to name God El Roi—"the God who sees."

What Hagar could say of God *we* can also say of him. He is the God who sees. He sees what we're running from, what has us down.

Is it a broken relationship?

Is it abuse from your past?

Is it a secret sin you're struggling with?

Is it that the bills are piling up and you don't know when relief is going to come?

Is it a miscarriage?

Or the inability to get pregnant?

Is it an addiction?

Is it an illness or injury?

Is it the death of a loved one?

God sees. He sees what we are going through, and it matters to him. This is why Peter told Christians, "Cast all your anxiety on him because he cares for you" (1 Peter 5:7).

BOTTLED TEARS

There is a Bible verse I've read many times that took on a new meaning for me after I learned of Zac's death. I've thought often about how it relates to his wife, Kelly.

> You keep track of all my sorrows.
> > You have collected all my tears in your bottle. (Psalm 56:8, NLT)

I've been a pastor long enough to know that when tragedy strikes and someone is experiencing grief and heartache, there's nothing anyone can say to make things better. We want to say something because it's human nature. We love our friends. We don't want them to hurt. We want them to know God has not forgotten them.

But saying something isn't usually the answer. Kelly doesn't need me or anyone else to tell her anything. I bet that no matter what has you down or is causing you to question whether God really sees you, someone telling you something isn't going to help you either.

Maybe, though, painting a word picture would help. This is what the psalmist was doing.

Those tears you are crying—God sees them and is keeping every one of them in a bottle.

The continual twisting and turning on your bed—he sees you and knows exactly what is keeping you awake.

I mentioned that the end of *Monsters, Inc.,* holds a surprise. Roz had been working as Mike and Sulley's boss so she could keep her eye on them, but she was actually an undercover agent for the Child Detection Agency. Mike and Sulley thought that they were on their own and that things were out of control, but the whole time, someone with power and authority was "always watching."

Someday you and I, Kelly and Ev, and all who have put their faith in Jesus will receive a surprise ending of how God works everything out. We will realize we were never alone. God was on our side and was working undercover, bringing together plans of which we were completely unaware.

That may help you right now. It may not. Either way, you can be sure of this: God is a God who sees. He sees you.

And I promise he *cares.*

CHAPTER 2

ALWAYS HEARING

~~~~~

*Does God really hear me? If so, what
about all my unanswered prayers?*

We were living our little version of the American dream.
I had an incredible job. I married way over my head.
Debbie and I had two beautiful daughters. Everything
was perfect—except the one thing that was missing.

I grew up with an older brother and younger sister and had
always planned to raise three children. I envisioned taking the
middle child's side in every argument (middle children unite!)
and figured there would be a special bond between us.

We had two kids, planned for three, and were so excited when
we learned Debbie was pregnant. We had smooth and easy preg-
nancies the first two times (by *we,* I mean Debbie), and the first
few weeks of the third pregnancy seemed to be more of the
same. Like all young expecting couples, we were praying for a
safe pregnancy, routine delivery, and healthy baby.

At our second checkup, as the doctor performed the sonogram, concern came over her face. She showed us what looked
almost like a halo around our baby and said, "There's a problem."

We set up our next appointment for three weeks later and
went home scared. We prayed and prayed for God to heal our
baby. We asked others to join us in prayer.

Every day, we wondered what was happening. I constantly

asked Debbie whether she noticed any changes internally. Of course, she didn't.

All we could do was pray and wait.

Pray and wait.

Pray and wait some more.

Finally, the day came for our follow-up appointment. I had that first-day-of-school sick feeling, as though my stomach had been invaded by a gang of angry butterflies riding Harleys. We walked in and were ushered back to the sonogram room. Debbie and I were both praying silently. Then, when the nurse left and we were waiting for the doctor, I took Debbie's hand and we prayed out loud together.

The door opened, and our doctor walked in. We exchanged some forced pleasantries, and then the doctor sat down and began the sonogram. We waited for what felt like forever but was probably only a few seconds. Then she said words that hit us like a ton of bricks.

"I'm sorry, but there is no heartbeat."

To say we were devastated is an understatement. For anyone who has experienced a miscarriage, you know what it's like.

We had felt so much joy about adding someone to our family. I was excited that Riley and Kelsey would have another sibling. We had let everyone know. We'd picked a name. We'd begun working on the nursery.

Now there was . . . *this*. Complete sadness. Conversations I never thought we'd have. I will never forget trying to explain to six-year-old Riley that our baby was sick and not going to be born.

The emotional trauma was intense. Like a punch in the gut, it took our breath away. We had prayed for our baby's health. *So* many people had prayed for our baby's health. I knew God is all-powerful and could protect and heal our baby. There is no degree of difficulty when it comes to God's miracles. It would have been

easy for him to do it, right? Isn't that what I preach? What I believe? But he hadn't.

Why?

We had prayed. Maybe, somehow, he just didn't hear us.

CALLER ID

I love the caller ID function on our cell phones. When my phone
rings, I typically know exactly who is calling because the person
is listed in my contacts.

I see his name.

I see his number.

I answer the phone.

If the person calling is not in my contacts, there is a 99.5 percent chance the call is going to voice mail. Don't roll your eyes
and judge me. You know you do the same thing!

Whenever we don't take a call, it's known as a call block.

Have you ever felt like God was call blocking you when you
prayed to him? I have. That's exactly how I felt when he didn't
answer our prayers for our baby's health.

Because you are reading this book, you probably believe that
God invites us to pray. I wonder, though, Do you believe that he
is listening?

I bet you answered yes. Why would God invite us to pray if he
wasn't going to listen? Of course he hears us.

But do you *really* feel that? I know we believe it, but do you *feel*
it? When you pray, do you feel like God is listening?

I'll ask it a different way: How do you *experience* God listening?
If someone asked you what it feels like when God listens to you,
how would you describe it? If you struggle to describe it, is it possible that God hearing you is something you believe in your head
but not so much in your heart?

Let me ask another question. (Sorry, I'm going to keep poking.)

If we believe God's listening, why don't we pray more? I know we have excuses: "I'm too busy," "My mind wanders when I pray," or "I don't know what to pray for." I say the same things. But wouldn't all our excuses dissolve if we really believed that God always hears? I mean, to have access to the all-knowing, all-powerful God of the universe, to be able to talk to him—if we really believed he's listening, wouldn't it be difficult to do anything other than pray?

One last question: If we pray because we do believe God is listening, why doesn't it always feel like it's working? Why can my wife and I pray to a God who loves us and hears us, ask him to save our baby, and get nothing but silence and heartache?

That unanswered prayer for our baby's health led me on a quest to make sure that God is always hearing. I opened my Bible, seeking answers.

Let's see if we can figure this out. We'll start with something we may take for granted: the amazing invitation we have from God to pray.

THE INVITATION

Former president George W. Bush, Peyton Manning, and Tim Tebow.

No, that is not the beginning of a "Three guys walk into a bar" joke. They are three people I have actually met in person! Why? I was invited! I don't want to brag, but I have been invited to events in which I met each of those esteemed men. I was intimidated to attend—remember, fam from Mississippi, grew up in Louisiana, college in Arkansas, never the smartest person in the room—but I went because I was invited.

I have also been invited to sit courtside at Mavericks games, to sit in box seats for the Cowboys, and to attend opening day for the Texas Rangers. Now, that I have moved to Houston I am waiting on my invite to watch the Rockets, Texans, and Astros.

I've been invited to share the gospel in countries as far south as Brazil and as far east as India.

When I step back, I can't believe I've had those opportunities!

But none of those is the most incredible invitation I have ever received. That invite came when I was thirteen years old.

It happened on Thanksgiving. I loved Thanksgiving as a kid because my family always had close relatives or friends over. The smell of Mom's home cooking filled the house as dishes of food started to cover the table. The *adult* table.

I was at the kiddie table. We kids were relegated to a make-shift table in a different room. We had to load up our plates at the adult table and then take the walk of shame away from the important conversations our parents were having.

I remember when I was finally the oldest kid at the kiddie table. Not. Cool. That's when it happened. I wasn't expecting it, but I was invited to come to the adult table. What?! Never had I felt so much pride. I might as well have been called up to the major leagues. I was so nervous! If you mess up the conversation or use the wrong fork, do you get sent back to the kiddie table?

To this day, next to the invitation to trust in Jesus, it's the best invitation I've ever received.

Well, I guess that would make it the *third*-best invitation because God invites us in the Bible to pray. Think about that! The almighty creator and sustainer of the universe, the God who was before it all and is above it all, wants *you* to talk to him. He says, "Call on me in the day of trouble; I will deliver you, and you will honor me" (Psalm 50:15) and "Call to me and I will answer you and tell you great and unsearchable things you do not know" (Jeremiah 33:3).

God tells us to "pray continually" (1 Thessalonians 5:17) and to "cast all [our] anxiety on him because he cares" for us (1 Peter 5:7).

It's incredible. God invites us to talk to him.

I can still remember when I first learned to pray. I think I was five years old. My dad got me out of my bed to kneel down next to him.

He showed me how to fold my hands with the fingers interlocking.

He taught me why bowing my head and closing my eyes were important.

Then he had me repeat a prayer with him. You're probably familiar with it: "Now I lay me down to sleep, I pray the Lord my soul to keep; if I should die before I wake, I pray the Lord my soul to take."

What the what?! If I *die* before I wake? The Lord is going to take my soul?! At five years old, my biggest concern was what flavor of ice cream to choose for dessert. My biggest fear was getting cooties from my sister. Now death was coming for me while I slept. It was terrifying! Who thought of teaching kids to pray this way?

Don't get me wrong. I'm grateful for a mom and dad who raised me to honor God and taught me how to pray, no matter how weird that first prayer was!

Looking back, I think about all the times the importance of prayer was reinforced in my life. From saying simple blessings at the dinner table to walking by the small prayer room in the church I grew up in, I knew from an early age that prayer is essential for Christians.

Why?

Because God has invited us to pray.

So, why does it seem that sometimes he doesn't hear us? As I set out on my journey to make sure that God is always hearing, the first question I had was whether we do anything to lead him to call block us.

BLOCKED CALLS

It turns out that there is a reason God will call block us. It's called *cherishing sin.*

The dictionary defines the word *cherish* as "to protect and care for (someone) lovingly; to hold (something) dear."[1]

I cherish my wife.

I cherish memories with my grandparents.

I'm *not* supposed to cherish sin. According to the psalmist, when I do, God won't listen to me. He blocks the call. "If I had cherished sin in my heart, the Lord would not have listened" (Psalm 66:18).

When we hold on to our sin as if it is a treasure to keep, our prayers become useless and ineffective. That feeling of our prayers not making it past the ceiling? They don't if we are cherishing sin.

Listen to what the prophet Isaiah had to say about this:

> Surely the arm of the LORD is not too short to save,
>   nor his ear too dull to hear.
> But your iniquities have separated
>   you from your God;
> your sins have hidden his face from you,
>   so that he will not hear. (59:1–2)

We have a choice: we can cherish our sin, or we can cherish our relationship with God. If we choose the former, we can cry out to God all day long but it will never make a difference. God will call block us every time.

So, if God seems silent, begin with a thorough search of your heart. Are you holding on to a sin?

Are you refusing to forgive someone who offended you?

Is the sin a lust or impurity of some kind?

Know this: God *never* call blocks someone who is sincerely seeking him and crying out to him.

Remember, he sees our hearts.

He discerns our motives.

He knows whether someone is legitimately and humbly calling to him in prayer.

When we call him from a sincere heart, he *always* takes the call. God always hears.

DROPPED CALLS

Dropped calls are so frustrating.

I was on the phone with a pastor friend of mine recently. He was asking for my opinion about someone he was looking to potentially hire. I shared the candidate's strengths and warned about a few weaknesses. I was going on and on when I finally realized that my buddy was no longer listening. He had driven through a dead spot, and the call was dropped.

Does something similar happen when you pray? You are talking to God about a need in your life but start to wonder if the call was dropped. Is it possible God is no longer listening?

There is a Bible verse that has always amazed me. It occurs when Jesus was in the middle of his ministry. He returned to Nazareth, the town he grew up in. The people of Nazareth knew Jesus.

He was a carpenter's son.

James, Joseph, Simon, and Judas's brother.

Mary's little boy.

The people of Nazareth had watched Jesus grow up. That was the issue. We know that familiarity can breed contempt. They knew Jesus. Jesus was not that big of a deal. Why all the fuss?

Jesus was rejected in his own hometown. Matthew recorded, "He did not do many mighty works there, because of their unbelief" (13:58, ESV).

Unbelief can cause a dropped call.

Why? Because unbelief is rooted in pride, and pride is the root of all sin. Pride feeds unbelief, and unbelief cuts us off from God.

James, a half brother of Jesus, was probably there in Nazareth that day. He was likely embarrassed by his brother's actions and teachings. Earlier in Jesus's ministry, we see James and the rest of Jesus's family sending for him, thinking that he was "out of his mind" (Mark 3:21).

It is interesting that Jesus's own family had trouble believing in him!

We know that after the Resurrection, James started to believe in Jesus. (Your brother rising from the dead will do that to you!) He didn't just believe; he became a leader in the early church. Church historians consider him one of the pillars of the Jerusalem church. An early-church tradition tells us that he was given the nickname Old Camel Knees because his knees were hard like a camel's due to the amount of time he spent kneeling in prayer.[2]

James went from unbelief to belief. He knew the danger that came with unbelief. Maybe this is why he wrote,

> If any of you lacks wisdom, you should ask God, who gives generously to all without finding fault, and it will be given to you. But when you ask, you must believe and not doubt, because the one who doubts is like a wave of the sea, blown and tossed by the wind. That person should not expect to receive anything from the Lord. (James 1:5–7)

James knew that unbelief can cause a dropped call in our prayer lives.

To be clear, God understands your doubts. We see Jesus dealing with people who were struggling with doubt—a fearful father, John the Baptist when he was in prison, Thomas after the Resurrection—and he graciously met them where they were and helped build their faith. God does not reject someone who is struggling with honest doubts. But a stubborn refusal to believe? That will cause a dropped call.

A CASE STUDY

I discovered some things we can do that might prevent God from hearing our prayers. Next, I wondered what we can do that might *help* God hear our prayers.

Researchers in different fields and professions often perform case studies to help give analysis and reveal valuable information regarding a particular question they are seeking to answer. When it comes to God hearing our prayers, perhaps a good case study will give us some insight.

Let's look at the life of a man named Hezekiah from the Old Testament. We are given two prayers that Hezekiah offered to God. One had to do with a national crisis he was confronting as the king of Judah; the other had to do with a personal health crisis.

In both instances, Hezekiah prayed to God and God heard his prayer.

What can we learn from the way Hezekiah prayed? Did he do anything special that caused God to hear his prayers?

Proximity Matters

Hezekiah was twenty-five years old when he became king of the divided kingdom of Judah. Most of Israel's kings were evil, but Hezekiah was different. Listen to how the Bible describes him:

> Hezekiah trusted in the LORD, the God of Israel. There was no one like him among all the kings of Judah, either before him or after him. He held fast to the LORD and did not stop

following him; he kept the commands the LORD had given Moses. (2 Kings 18:5–6)

The character of Hezekiah is worth noting. His morality might not have made the Lord hear his prayer, but I bet it didn't hurt. If we were to take a deeper look at Hezekiah's character, we would find that it was directly tied to his relationship with the Lord.

Hezekiah trusted in the Lord. He had integrity, and he also had faith. It was his faith that led him to stay close to God.

The following may be obvious, but it's a principle I imagine needs to be reinforced: *proximity matters.* I'm not talking about physical distance. God took care of that when he gave his Holy Spirit. He is viscerally present to—and even in—every believer.

By proximity, I'm talking about intimacy. How close we are to God determines whether or not he listens to our prayers.

This makes sense, doesn't it? It's kind of like my kids trying to get my attention from their rooms upstairs. They don't want to walk down the stairs to talk. So, what do they do? They scream. They yell.

We just can't have a conversation that way. I can barely hear them calling my name. Why? The distance is too great, and they are too distracted.

They don't want to push pause on the show they're watching.

They have friends they're texting.

They have social media to keep an eye on.

Do you see the parallel? We want God to hear our prayers, but we never draw close to him. Unlike Hezekiah, we're not following him and striving to keep his commandments. We're distracted with other things and wonder why God isn't hearing us.

Why?

Proximity matters.

Posture Matters

My wife and I often teach the premarital classes our church offers. We have also been called on to speak at different events centered on building strong marriages. We always enjoy the opportunity to invest in couples and do what we can to help them grow in their relationship with each other.

We came up with a "Ten Commandments to a Quality Marriage" talk together. Commandment number six is "Thou shalt learn to Tebow."

Before Tim Tebow ever tried to make it in major-league baseball, he was making it in the NFL. When he played for the Denver Broncos, hardly anyone really gave Tim Tebow a chance until they had to. The former Heisman Trophy winner was the backup quarterback in 2011 until the sixth game of the season.

He took over the 1–4 Broncos, leading them on numerous fourth-quarter comebacks and ultimately to the AFC West title and first playoff win in six years.[3] You would think that these accomplishments would have garnered the most news about him, but instead the media seemed to be infatuated with his kneeling in prayer before, during, and after games. They actually coined it "Tebowing."[4]

The sixth commandment that Debbie and I teach on is all about the importance of a married couple praying together. *Tebowing* refers to getting on your knees—well, Tim usually got on one knee (I can call him Tim because, remember, I met him!)—and praying. It has to do with posture. And although posture may not make God hear us any clearer or listen any closer, it does show him that we're serious about what we're doing.

Author and pastor Mark Batterson wrote in his book *The Circle Maker,*

Physical posture is an important part of prayer. It's like a prayer within a prayer. Posture is to prayer as tone is to communication. If words are what you say, then posture is how you say it. . . . Physical postures help posture our hearts and minds.[5]

People in the Bible prayed in a number of different ways. Some prayed while sitting. Others prayed while standing. Some prayed with their hands lifted in the air. Others prayed while pacing back and forth. We even see that some people prayed while lying prostrate with their faces bowed to the ground.[6]

Physical posture can be a reflection of our hearts' posture. God listens to prayers, but it seems he leans in closer when they flow out of the humility within our hearts. Peter wrote, "God opposes the proud but gives grace to the humble" (1 Peter 5:5, ESV).

Hezekiah showed his humility with how he postured himself before God. When the king of Assyria sent a letter to Hezekiah warning him of an impending war and threatening to overtake Jerusalem, Hezekiah "went up to the temple of the LORD and spread it out before the LORD. And Hezekiah prayed to the LORD" (2 Kings 19:14–15).

When Isaiah the prophet told Hezekiah he would die, confronting him with his own mortality, notice how he responded: "Hezekiah turned his face to the wall and prayed to the LORD. . . . And Hezekiah wept bitterly" (20:2–3).

On both occasions, Hezekiah modeled humility. It was the posture of his heart.

I have noticed that broken people are humble people. God is attracted to and always hears broken, humble people. That includes you. When you feel insecure or unworthy, you can go to God, knowing he will be drawn to you. He promises he "is close to the brokenhearted and saves those who are crushed in spirit" (Psalm 34:18). Maybe those times when you're most embarrassed to pray to him are the times when he's actually most excited to hear from you. Why? Think of a kid who does something stupid and embarrassing in front of a crowd. She feels ashamed, but her parent wants nothing more than to hold her in that moment. There is no sin, no shame, and no force on earth or from hell that can come between you and your loving and listening Father.

Hezekiah knew he could not defend Jerusalem against the king of Assyria. He didn't have the manpower or the expertise to lead his nation to victory over a stronger adversary. After being told he would not recover from his sickness, he knew there was nothing he could physically do to make himself better.

Both of these instances led to brokenness. In the first instance, Hezekiah ran to the temple to pray. In the second, he turned on his bed to face the wall and wept, and then he did the one thing, the *only* thing, he could do: he prayed.

Proximity matters.

Posture matters.

Perspective Matters

Hezekiah was very clear about whom he directed his prayers to.

> Hezekiah prayed to the LORD: *"LORD, the God of Israel, enthroned between the cherubim, you alone are God over all the kingdoms of the earth. You have made heaven and earth."* (2 Kings 19:15, emphasis added)

Hezekiah acknowledged God's sovereignty. He confessed his awareness of the fact that God is all-powerful and in control. Hezekiah knew that God could do what he could not. And here is the key: *Hezekiah trusted God no matter what God decided.*

When the king of Assyria was coming against him, Hezekiah prayed and asked God to intervene. When he was warned that he would not overcome his sickness and would die, he prayed and asked God to intervene.

In both situations, he demonstrated trust in God. In both situations, God heard his prayer.

He had no idea *how* God would intervene. An angel going through the Assyrian camp and killing 185,000 soldiers? Probably not how he was expecting God to answer his prayer.

What about his health? Hezekiah was thirty-nine years old when Isaiah told him to get his affairs in order because he was about to die. Hezekiah prayed and God restored his health, adding fifteen more years to his life.

I'm forty-two years old at the time of this writing. Fifteen more years is great, but I'll be only fifty-seven years old then. If I were in Hezekiah's place, I'd be thinking, *Thank you, Lord, for the extra years, but can't you do a little more?* I would probably be doing a bit more debating about how much extra time he was giving me.

Not Hezekiah. He trusted the Lord.

It reminds me of Jesus in the Garden of Gethsemane the night he was betrayed and arrested. Do you remember the scene?

Jesus asked his best friends to pray with him that evening, but they kept falling asleep. What lay ahead for Jesus was weighing heavily on him emotionally and spiritually. He was sweating drops of blood as he prayed, asking God to show him a different route to take than the cross (Matthew 26:36–46).

But there was no other way. Jesus taught us an important lesson in the garden. He taught us to pray for God's will to be done instead of our own. Only someone with a deep trust in God can pray this prayer and actually mean it.

When we trust God like that and pray like that, his silence doesn't scare us.

We know he hears us.

He *always* hears us.

We just have to learn to wait and keep our trust in him.

"CONGRATULATIONS!"

Just days after the doctor told us that our baby had no heartbeat, we had to go to the hospital so Debbie could deliver our stillborn child. There was so much grief. As we checked into the labor-and-delivery wing, I thought, *This is supposed to be the wing of the hospital where there is so much happiness and joy.*

Not for us. It was just pain.

In the midst of this, all I knew to do was pray. I didn't understand why God was allowing this to happen. It broke my heart to wake up in the middle of the night feeling the bed shake because of my wife's crying.

I was at a loss. I didn't know how to help besides pray. I couldn't understand why God had not answered our prayers for our baby's health, but I just kept trusting him. It wasn't easy. I had to fight for it. I fought, and I continued praying. I prayed for my wife. I prayed for our kids. We still wanted to have another child, so I prayed for that too.

On the anniversary of our hearing the words "I'm sorry, but there is no heartbeat," we found ourselves back with the same doctor. That day, she turned to us and we heard these words: "Congratulations! There are *two* heartbeats. Are you ready to have two more in your family?"

Twins.

Amazing. Just like God. We left that day in awe of God hearing our prayers. And not just hearing but *answering* them in a way only he could. A double blessing. Literally.

If you ask me why he did not answer our prayers the first time around, I will tell you the truth: I don't know.

I have other prayers that he has not answered the way I wanted. I actually have *many* prayers that he hasn't answered the way I hoped he would. I don't know why. I may never know why.

I don't have answers, but I do have faith. It seems like just barely enough sometimes, but I do have faith.

I choose to trust. Like Jesus in the garden, I want God's will, not mine.

If you embrace the kind of radical surrender Jesus did—telling God, "I want what you want more than what I want"—can you imagine the kind of freedom and peace you will have? Picture a confused new driver with only a learner's permit trying to weave through fast-moving traffic and having no idea if he's even going in the right direction. Imagine him stopping, scooting over into the passenger's seat, and giving the steering wheel to a professional driver with a finely tuned GPS. Whew! The pressure is now off, and the tension is a thing of the past. That could be *you* if you'd just let God drive. "Not my will, but yours be done" (Luke 22:42). You can do that. You just need to trust him.

I trust him.

He's invited me to pray.

I know the always God *always hears* me.

CHAPTER 3

ALWAYS SPEAKING

~~~~~~

Does God really speak? I'm listening,
so if he's speaking, I don't get it.

You've been there, right?

I have. It usually happens late at night or early in the morning. I'm by myself, either sitting dejected in my favorite chair or walking aimlessly through the house. I should be praying, but I'm not. I'm pacing instead. So much is on my mind and heart.

I should be praying because I really need God. I'm stuck in a confusing situation, and I desperately need wisdom. Or I am feeling overwhelmed and need to hear some encouraging words from God. Or I have a big decision to make, and all I want is for God to give me some direction.

So, why am I not praying? Because I don't need to speak to God; I need him to speak to me. And if I'm being totally honest—remember, we promised we would be—I'm just not confident that he's going to speak. Or maybe he is speaking and I'm just not good at hearing his voice.

Have you been there, sitting alone in that favorite chair, wondering how to get God to speak to you? It's such a big deal. If we don't hear his voice, we lack the wisdom, encouragement, and direction we need. We may make bad decisions. We may feel like giving up.

Hearing God speak is at the heart of a relationship with him. It's all about his voice.

THE VOICE

The voice is *so* important.

One of my family's favorite reality shows is *The Voice*. Vocalists from across the United States try to win a singing competition that is based solely on the performers' voices. Unlike the show *The Masked Singer*, those performing are not celebrities. The show is also different from *American Idol* because in the audition round of *The Voice*, the judges' chairs face the audience rather than the performer. The judges can't see the singer. It's the singer's voice that gets their attention.

Any judges who like the sound of the voice hit buttons that spin their chairs so they can see the person singing. The performer then gets to pick which one of the turned judges she wants to be coached by, and the journey begins.

From blind auditions to battle rounds and knockouts and then live performances, performers try to get to the next round each week until ultimately the television audience chooses the winner, designating one person to have *the voice*.

This show comes to mind when I think about God speaking. The Bible teaches that God does still speak, and God's voice is *so* important.

In a world filled with so much noise, with so many competing voices, Jesus tells us that we know and follow him by recognizing his voice (John 10:2–16). When you need to be encouraged, when you don't know what to do, when you need wisdom, or when you're not sure which way to turn, it's all about the voice.

But we often struggle to hear God speak. One issue that can make this challenging is that we cannot see God. So, I wonder, since our chairs are turned around, how do we hear God's voice, and is it even possible to *really* know his voice?

EXPERIENCING GOD

I first went through Henry Blackaby and Claude King's bestselling workbook, *Experiencing God,* when I was in eighth grade. First released in 1990, it has sold more than seven million copies and has been published in forty-five languages around the world.[1] It took evangelical churches by storm, and churches like mine considered it to be the next-best thing to the Bible.

Football teams have their playbooks.

Actors and actresses have their scripts.

Evangelicals have the Bible and *Experiencing God.*

Recently, I was going through some boxes while cleaning out a closet in my office and I came across an old blank *Experiencing God* workbook. I had such great memories of working through it nearly thirty years ago that I figured I would take this copy home and start all over again. It didn't take long before I read these words: "If you have trouble hearing God speak, you are in trouble at the very heart of your Christian experience."[2]

Wow. Think about that in relation to your own Christian experience. Are you hearing God speak? When was the last time you heard his voice? Are Blackaby and King right? I began to review my own journey with the Lord. When in my life was I confident that God was speaking to me?

The Bible is clear: God speaks. Nine times in the very first chapter of the first book of the Bible, we read the phrase "And God said." Throughout the Old Testament, we read about God talking to his people, Israel, by continually speaking directly to them and through different prophets, priests, and kings.

God spoke to Moses. The Bible says, "The LORD would speak to Moses face to face, as one speaks to a friend" (Exodus 33:11).

I wonder what that was like?

Moses first heard the voice of God on the backside of a desert when he was eighty years old. Remember the story? He was raised in the lap of luxury in Pharaoh's family after being adopted as an infant. He had all the privileges and pleasures Egypt had to offer, but as he grew in age and matured, he knew he was different. He was a Hebrew. Hebrews were slaves in Egypt.

One day, he saw a Hebrew being beaten by an Egyptian. Something must have snapped inside him, because Moses went over to the altercation and killed the Egyptian, burying him in the sand. The next day, he went out again and saw two Hebrews fighting each other. After Moses tried to break up the fight, one of them called Moses out on his murder of the Egyptian the day before. Moses knew he was found out. He had to leave Egypt.

In fear, he ran away. As far as he could. He ended up in a place called Midian. Moses met his wife in Midian. He became a shepherd and, for the next forty years, labored on the backside of nowhere.

I bet Moses thought often about what happened all those years ago. Watching sheep couldn't have been that exciting. My only experience in watching sheep has put me to sleep! I have to imagine he had plenty of time to wonder how the family who raised him was doing. Did his family remember him? Miss him? Think of him?

Surely, he thought about his people, the Hebrews. For his whole life, they had been slaves to the Egyptians. He must have wondered if they were still as bad off as they were when he ran away all those years ago.

The Bible gives us a little insight into what was going on during this time, and I think it's pretty relevant for what we have covered so far in this book.

> During those many days the king of Egypt died, and the people of Israel groaned because of their slavery and cried out for help. Their cry for rescue from slavery came up to God. And God heard their groaning, and God remembered his covenant with Abraham, with Isaac, and with Jacob. God saw the people of Israel—and God knew. (2:23–25, ESV)

Did you catch that? Read those verses again very slowly. Amazing! Look at these phrases:

God heard.
God remembered.
God saw.
God knew.

These four phrases may be all you really need to grasp. These four phrases may have been worth the price of this book.

Think about each of them.

God *heard*. God hears your cry. Whatever is bothering you and holding you back, whatever is a burden to you and breaking your heart, just cry out to God. He hears.

God *remembered*. He's not like us! He doesn't need to set multiple reminders on his iPhone. God has not aged and gotten forgetful in his elderly years. He remembers you and the promises he has made to you. He remembers.

God *saw*. We spent a whole chapter on this one concept. The God who watches over you does not slumber or sleep. Nothing gets past him. Nothing. He sees.

God *knew*. God is fully aware of every situation and circumstance you find yourself in. He knows what will happen. He knows when it will happen. Nothing takes him by surprise. As I've heard it asked, "Has it ever occurred to you that nothing has ever occurred to God?" He knows.

God hears, remembers, sees, and knows. The question we are asking is, Does God *speak*? So, remember, Moses was counting sheep in the middle of nowhere.

Moses was tending the flock of Jethro his father-in-law, the priest of Midian, and he led the flock to the far side of the wilderness and came to Horeb, the mountain of God. There the angel of the LORD appeared to him in flames of

fire from within a bush. Moses saw that though the bush
was on fire it did not burn up. So Moses thought, "I will go
over and see this strange sight—why the bush does not
burn up."

When the LORD saw that he had gone over to look, God
called to him from within the bush, "Moses! Moses!"

And Moses said, "Here I am." (Exodus 3:1–4)

What a sight this must have been to Moses! A bush on fire is
not that big of a deal. But a bush on fire and not consumed by the
fire? Moses turned toward the bush and heard the voice of God.

In *Experiencing God,* Blackaby and King used this Exodus passage to give four distinguishing marks of God speaking. I think
their comments will help us as we consider how God speaks to us
today.

First, they wrote, "When God spoke, it was usually unique to
that individual."[3] In other words, God didn't speak to Abraham
the same way he spoke to Moses or Elijah or Samuel. This is important because it demonstrates that God is not limited in how
he communicates.

In the Old Testament, he spoke through a donkey! Some people who listen to me preach say he *still* speaks through donkeys
today! God is not boxed in, in how he communicates.

How amazing is that? God loves you so much that he wants to
speak to you in a way that is unique to you, that will get your attention and make sense to you.

Second, "when God spoke, the person was sure God was
speaking."[4] God introduced himself to Moses a few verses later in
this passage of Scripture as "the God of your father, the God of
Abraham, the God of Isaac and the God of Jacob." (verse 6).
Later, God would clarify that he is the "I AM" (verse 14)—the self-
existent, eternal, ever-present God of the universe. Moses would
respond by removing his shoes and hiding his face. He did not

have to question or doubt who was speaking to him. He knew it was God.

Third, "when God spoke, the person knew what God said."[5] There was certainty surrounding what God was communicating to Moses. "Come, I will send you to Pharaoh that you may bring my people, the children of Israel, out of Egypt" (verse 10, ESV). Moses may have doubted he was up for the job, but there was no question as to what the job was. God spoke and was very clear in his communication.

Fourth, "when God spoke, that was the encounter with God."[6] The burning bush was not a coincidence. Moses didn't need to look behind door number two to experience God. God speaking to him was the experience!

Now, if you are like me, your immediate thought is, *Jarrett, that's Moses. God doesn't speak to people today like he did to Moses and others in the Bible.*

Trust me, I get it. I've often wondered what I would do if I heard the audible voice of God.

THE LIGHTHOUSE

I have a confession: I am a church nerd. For some reason, I have always loved the church. People who love to work out are often called gym rats. They stay in the gym for hours working out or, if they play basketball, working on their jump shots. Well, I am a self-confessing church rat.

My earliest memories are from the church. For as long as I can remember, I have felt at home in the church. I love everything about it. I love the hymns. I love the old wooden pews. I love the snacks they would give us kids. I can't tell you when I missed a Vacation Bible School or church summer camp as a child.

In fact, at the time of this writing, I will have missed only one church summer camp in the past thirty years of my life. You read

that right. I have either been a camper or served as a camp counselor or camp pastor for three decades now.

My very first church camp was a preteen camp when I was
eleven years old. This was when I sensed God speaking to me for
the very first time.

Clara Springs Baptist Camp is in the small town of Pelican,
Louisiana. When I say *small*, I mean really small. Population 725
people small. You've heard of a one-stoplight town? This was a
one-*road* town. People from there would give you directions to
their home by saying, "My house is the one on the left."

For my first church-camp experience, though, it was awesome. What's better than hanging out with your friends for an
entire week without your parents?

We did what every church camp does. We swam (guys and
girls separated, of course!). We had games to play and sports as
electives. We had small-group-discipleship time and worship at
night. And being preteen kids, showers that week were probably
optional. (Today, when I go to our church's preteen camp every
year, I'm still haunted by the musky odor that comes from some
of those dorm rooms.)

Back then, our camp pastor for the week had his work cut out
for him. How do you keep the attention of a few hundred preteen kids? Well, this guy had it down.

He was an artist, and he would draw a picture with chalk as he
preached. Toward the end of the message, he would turn on a
fluorescent black light, and an image we had not yet seen appeared. It was incredible.

One night he drew a picture of an unbelievable mountainside,
and when he turned on the black light at the end of the message,
a huge eagle appeared, flying through the sky. Nearly thirty years
later, I can still recall the pastor's message of how God can renew
our strength like an eagle's.

Another night, he drew a picture of the scene at Calvary. He

told the story of Jesus dying on the cross for our sins. The drawing that night seemed so dark. When he turned the black light
on, the picture went from dark and gloomy to bright and colorful
with an image of Jesus ascending into the sky. He preached that
night on the death, resurrection, and ascension of Jesus.

My eleven-year-old self was captivated. Although I loved all
the fun we were having at camp during the day, I could not wait
for evening worship to see what the camp pastor would do next.

I will never forget the second-to-last night of camp. I even remember the date: August 3, 1989.

The pastor drew a picture of what appeared to be an ocean in
an uproar. He then drew a boat being tossed by the waves. It was
easy to see that the boat was having trouble and nearly going
under.

On the far side of the picture was a small cliff and, on top of
the cliff, a lighthouse. The pastor began to speak about how this
picture represented some of our lives. He talked about how even
as young kids we could have doubts and struggle with fears. He
mentioned how sin could sink our lives and how only Jesus could
save us.

The pastor turned on the black light, and an image of Jesus's
face appeared looking over the boat being rocked by the waves.
The lighthouse in the corner lit up, casting a light over the length
of the picture.

It was amazing—not just the picture but the message. It was
like he was reading my mail. Well, as an eleven-year-old, I didn't
have mail. I guess it was more like he was going through my
Trapper Keeper from school!

I wasn't a bad kid who messed up in any major ways. But on
the inside, I felt like that boat looked. I knew sin was the problem,
and I knew Jesus was the lighthouse that would get me to safety
and refuge.

That night, I made the decision to put my faith and trust in

Jesus. When the pastor gave an invitation to respond to his message, I can't describe it, but I *knew* God was speaking to me and leading me to respond. It wasn't an audible voice, but there was no mistaking it: he was speaking.

I'll never forget it. What's really cool is that two days later, when the camp ended, I was named camper of the year. (I was camper of the year the next summer too, but who's counting?) Want to know my reward for winning camper of the year? I got to pick one drawing the camp pastor did that week to take home with me. Would you like to guess which one I picked?

I had the lighthouse drawing framed and hung in my bedroom in the house where I grew up. It stayed there until just recently. I always knew that I wanted it in my study. A few years ago, when my wife and I bought our home, the first call I made was to my dad to get the picture ready. As I write this, I can look on the wall to my left and see it hanging there.

It's a constant reminder to me that God still speaks. And when he does, you will know that it's him speaking.

Jesus said, "My sheep hear my voice, and I know them, and they follow me" (John 10:27, ESV).

God is still speaking. It's probably not going to be audible or in a burning bush, like it was for Moses. It might not be through a chalk talk, like it was for me when I was eleven years old. But God is still speaking.

LOST IN TRANSLATION

As I've mentioned, I have had the privilege of traveling to and preaching the gospel in the jungles of the Amazon River basin in Brazil and on the far eastern coast of India. I've preached in major cities around the world, such as Bucharest, Romania, and Cologne, Germany.

Every time I preach in one of these places, I have to use an interpreter. It's not as easy as you might think.

First, you have to organize your time well. If you are given forty minutes to speak, you can share only about twenty minutes' worth of content. You have to give your interpreter an equal amount of time to translate what you are attempting to communicate. Second—and I've learned this the hard way—humor and some analogies can sometimes not translate well. When I preach in the jungles of the Amazon, saying "God will wash your sins as white as snow" means nothing. The people who live there have never seen snow! Third, simplicity is always best.

If you miss any of these key steps, there is a chance that what you are saying will get lost in translation. You are speaking and people are listening, but they have no idea what you are saying.

I think this is how it is with God sometimes. He is attempting to communicate with us, but because of our sin or the fact that we just aren't paying attention, we may have no idea what he is saying. We might not hear his voice at all, and his voice is *so* important.

Remember, Jesus said we will know and follow him by recognizing his voice. It's all about the voice. But so often we struggle to know whether God is speaking and to discern what he's saying.

So, let's look at some ways in which he speaks so we can make sure we turn our chairs when we hear his voice. We'll start with how he speaks generally to all people and then make our way through how he speaks more specifically to individuals who follow him.

God Speaks Through His *Creation*

I've heard people say, "If God existed, I wish he would just write it in the sky. Then I would believe." Well, then, good news: he has written it in the sky!

> The heavens declare the glory of God;
> the skies proclaim the work of his hands.

Day after day they pour forth speech;
    night after night they reveal knowledge. (Psalm 19:1–2)

Standing before the vastness of the ocean as the sun is setting or peering up from the base of a mountain or staring into a starlit sky, if you are quiet and reflective enough, it won't take long for you to understand that God is speaking through his creation.

He is attempting to get your attention.

I've seen images of all four of my children prebirth and been present at each of their births. How anyone can see a baby being formed in the womb, hear his heartbeat, or see him take his first breath and ignore the voice of God speaking is beyond me.

Let's be clear: God speaks through creation. If we don't hear him, it is because our hearts have become hard and our hearing dull. He is speaking; we just may not want to hear it. Paul wrote to the church in Rome about this.

> The wrath of God is being revealed from heaven against all the godlessness and wickedness of people, who suppress the truth by their wickedness, since what may be known about God is plain to them, because God has made it plain to them. For since the creation of the world God's invisible qualities—his eternal power and divine nature—have been clearly seen, being understood from what has been made, so that people are without excuse. (Romans 1:18–20)

God speaks to us through his creation. In creation, he shows us that he values diversity and order and consistency and beauty.

As author and speaker Rebecca Barlow Jordan wrote, "By observing the ant's strength to store up food all summer long, we learn about wisdom and industriousness. . . . And through planting and growing a garden, we 'hear' about miracles of death and rebirth."[7]

Place your finger on your pulse. Feel your heart beating.

As you take a deep breath, feel how your lungs fill with oxygen.

We can't control how our bodies do either of these things. Internally, we know we are not the rulers of our domains. There is the Creator, and he is speaking to us through his creation.

God Speaks Through Our Consciences

Paul, again writing to the church in Rome, said,

> When Gentiles, who do not have the law, do by nature things required by the law, they are a law for themselves, even though they do not have the law. They show that the requirements of the law are written on their hearts, their consciences also bearing witness, and their thoughts sometimes accusing them and at other times even defending them. (2:14–15)

There is no doubt that God speaks to us through our consciences and has written eternity on every one of our souls. Solomon, the wisest man to ever live, wrote, "He has put eternity into man's heart" (Ecclesiastes 3:11, ESV).

Sit still long enough, be quiet long enough, and your conscience will bear witness to the fact that you know the difference between right and wrong. Innate within you is a desire for justice to take place and wrongs to be made right. You have a desire within you that this world and all its successes and affluence cannot fill.

You know these things not just because you were taught them as a child or learned them from experience but because God wrote them on your heart from the very beginning. It's just one of the ways he speaks to us.

Perhaps you have allowed sin to creep into your life. You've been ignoring it, accepting it, but a sense of conviction is tugging at your heart even as you read this sentence right now. That's God speaking to you through your conscience.

If you are struggling to hear him or to know what to do, here's another way he speaks. But it's one we have to be careful about.

God Speaks Through *Circumstances*

There have been reports of several earthquakes in the news recently. Is God speaking to us through these earthquakes? I would say, "Absolutely. In a number of ways."

He is speaking to us about the brevity of life. He is speaking to us about how we are not in control. He is speaking to us about helping those who have been affected by the earthquakes and are in need. Jesus told us that earthquakes would happen before he comes again, so in a way, he reminds us through these earthquakes that he is coming soon.

God will use circumstances and crises to get our attention.

It could be a worldwide pandemic.

It could be an unexpected diagnosis from a doctor.

It could be the sudden loss of a job.

God can use any type of circumstances to speak to us. Often, they are painful circumstances. For some reason, we tend to hear a little better in tough times. C. S. Lewis wrote, "God whispers to us in our pleasures, speaks in our conscience, but shouts in our pains: it is His megaphone to rouse a deaf world."[8]

God speaks to us through circumstances of all kinds, not just painful ones. When I was praying about pastoral ministry as a vocation, someone advised me, "If God is truly calling you to this, doors will begin to open and opportunities that were not there before will present themselves to you."

That person was exactly right. Once I decided to move forward in obedience to what God was calling me to do, I was invited to lead Bible studies and speak at events. He was speaking to me and affirming my call through circumstances that were outside my control.

For you, it may be a new job that has presented itself. Is God speaking to you about a transition through this new opportunity? I don't know. Certainly, not every circumstance is God speaking. This is where prayer, the Bible, the Holy Spirit, and wise counsel come in. Let's discuss these.

God Speaks Through *Prayer and the Bible*

We established in the previous chapter that God hears our prayers. But prayer is not just our speaking to God; it is also our allowing God to speak to us. God can whisper to us when we pray to him, and he always speaks when his Word is read.

I love that we don't have to guess at what God is saying because he has given us Scripture. His Word serves as his voice to us. Every time we read the Bible or listen to it being preached faithfully, we can know for sure that God is speaking.

The Bible is not an ordinary book: "The word of God is alive and active. Sharper than any double-edged sword, it penetrates even to dividing soul and spirit, joints and marrow; it judges the thoughts and attitudes of the heart" (Hebrews 4:12).

I like to tell people, "When we read the Bible, the Bible reads us." We can be certain that God is speaking every time we open the Scriptures.

Paul wrote to Timothy, "All Scripture is God-breathed and is useful for teaching, rebuking, correcting and training in righteousness, so that the servant of God may be thoroughly equipped for every good work" (2 Timothy 3:16–17).

God inspired every single word of the Bible. Jesus said that even "an iota" and "a dot" (Matthew 5:18, ESV) would remain forever. Think of an iota or a dot as a comma or an apostrophe in our English language.

The Bible is not going anywhere. "Heaven and earth will pass away, but my words will never pass away" (24:35).

Think about this as it relates to your own time alone with the Lord. Are you consistently reading God's Word? Are you really taking in what he has written to you?

I know so many people who want God to speak to them but they never open a Bible. Every time you open God's Word, you can be sure he is speaking. Don't fall into the trap of thinking Scripture was written by men and so it's full of mistakes and can't be trusted. Peter reminded believers, "Prophecy never had its origin in the human will, but prophets, though human, spoke from God as they were carried along by the Holy Spirit" (2 Peter 1:21).

I'm so grateful that God invites us to pray to him and gives us his Word as a sure way to hear his voice. But get this: God gets even *more* up close and personal in speaking to us.

God Speaks Through the *Holy Spirit*

The Holy Spirit's role is to glorify Jesus by taking what he has said and enabling us to understand and obey it. This is why the Bible calls him the Spirit of truth and our Helper. Jesus taught his disciples:

> When he, the Spirit of truth, comes, he will guide you into all the truth. He will not speak on his own; he will speak only what he hears, and he will tell you what is yet to come. He will glorify me because it is from me that he will receive what he will make known to you. (John 16:13–14)

God speaks to us by the Holy Spirit. It's important to remember that what God speaks through his Holy Spirit will *never* contradict his Word. They will *always* align.

You may have heard someone say, "God told me not to be

honest with my spouse" or "The Holy Spirit let me know that I don't need to go to church anymore." No. God would not tell someone either of those things because they contradict what he has already said in his Word.

The Holy Spirit enlightens us.

The Holy Spirit convicts us.

Perhaps you've heard the phrase *the still small voice of God*. This is the Holy Spirit. Don't be fooled, though: the still small voice is often louder and clearer than any audible voice you have ever heard.

I want to make sure you know one final way that God will speak to you. It's one we too often ignore.

God Speaks Through *Wise Counsel*

Solomon offered a number of proverbs that speak to the importance of listening to wise counsel:

> Where there is no guidance, a people falls,
>   but in an abundance of counselors there is safety. (11:14, ESV)

> Without counsel plans fail,
>   but with many advisers they succeed. (15:22, ESV)

> By wise guidance you can wage your war,
>   and in abundance of counselors there is victory. (24:6, ESV)

We all need friends who can help us discern whether or not God is speaking. This is why we all need biblical community through a local church.

Wise counsel helps especially in the gray issues of life. God clearly speaks to certain things in the Scriptures. They are laid out for us in his Word in black and white:

Avoid sexual immorality!

Give openhandedly! Be generous!

Love justice! Do mercy!

Keep the Ten Commandments—they are commandments,
  not suggestions!

Share the gospel!

These are things God has clearly told us in his Word.

But what about the gray areas?

Should I make this move to a new location?

Is it the right time for a career transition?

Do we move forward with this adoption?

Do I take the next step in this relationship?

What college should I attend?

Do I hit up Whataburger or In-N-Out? (Let me help you out:
  God is for both of these! And if you live in one of the
  thirty-six states without Whataburger or In-N-Out, may
  God have mercy on your soul.)

Gray areas are where God will use prayer, the Bible, the Holy Spirit, and wise counsel to help the most in discerning his voice.

God is *still* in the speaking business.

SILENCE

We can't close this chapter without addressing what I know some of you are thinking. In fact, you might be pretty frustrated with me.

You are living for Jesus in the best way you know how. You are reading his Word. You are in church and listening to the sermons your pastor preaches. Heck, you may even listen to podcasts of your favorite pastors from all over the country teaching the Bible. To the best of your ability, you are living to honor Jesus.

But regarding a specific situation you are facing, God seems to be silent. You are listening, but you just don't feel as if you are hearing from him.

You've sought wise counsel.

You've waited for clarity.

But God just doesn't seem to be speaking.

It's never fun to wait, is it?

If I want something, I Amazon Prime it so it will be here the next day.

If I need an app to help me with something, I can download it in less than a minute.

If I want to listen to a certain song on my playlist, I can play it as quickly as I can find it.

Why wait on dinner? Let's order an appetizer and get started!

We hate waiting. We want what we want, and we want it *now*. I'm sorry to have to tell you this, but God doesn't work that way. In his economy, waiting on him produces something that nothing else can produce.

Think back to our story of Moses. He labored in the wilderness for forty years before God ever spoke. He waited *forty years*!

I'm sure you're encouraged now and can't wait to leave a positive review on Amazon for me. Yeah, you're welcome.

Sometimes God has us wait. We need to trust him and his timing. We need to "wait for the LORD; be strong and take heart and wait for the LORD" (Psalm 27:14).

Look at what Moses was doing while he waited: "Moses was tending the flock of Jethro his father-in-law" (Exodus 3:1).

You know what Moses did while God was silent? He went about his daily routine. He kept sheep like he had every day for the past forty years. *Then* came his encounter with God. God's showing up and speaking changed the whole trajectory of Moses's life.

If you are in a period in which God seems to be silent, be like Moses. Oswald Chambers wrote in *My Utmost for His Highest*,

"Routine is God's way of saving us between our times of inspiration."[9] Keep engaging in your spiritual habits that keep you connected to God.

Keep waking up and reading your Bible.

Keep walking in biblical community and getting wise counsel.

Keep waiting on God and surrendering your life to him.

Keep doing what you are doing, and God *will* come through.

Be assured: the always God is *always speaking*. When he does, you will know that it's his voice. Just make sure to turn your chair.

ALWAYS WORKING

CHAPTER 4

PURSUING THE LOST

*Why isn't God pursuing this person I love
who is far from him?*

A disgusted "Save it" is not what I was hoping to hear.

What do you do when the person you're closest to is far from God? In fact, farther than far—what if he is absolutely *lost*? We had spent our entire lives together. What if we spent our eternal lives apart?

My brother, Eric, is three years older than me, and throughout our childhood, he was bigger than me and a talented athlete. I liked him and looked up to him, even though I never would have let him know it. When we were growing up, he would pick on me. I'm pretty sure he thought he had to—that it was somewhere toward the top of the big-brother job description. Yet if someone else tried to mess with me or bully me, he was the first to come to my defense.

Our mom and dad faithfully took us to church. We both "walked the aisle" to receive Christ at a very young age. We grew up going to the same Sunday school classes, church camps, and VBS programs. We could dissect and predict what would happen on a flannelgraph board better than Tony Romo can with a football game.

I was a sophomore when my brother graduated from high school and left for the University of Southern Mississippi. I felt like I was losing my lifelong buddy. It was heartbreaking, but at least I got to visit him with my folks. He even let me stay the night with him at his frat house. I'm still scarred by some of what I saw there!

The worst thing I witnessed was Eric himself. I discovered that he had embraced the partying lifestyle. He loved it. I thought that having him away from home was bad, but I was beginning to understand that it was actually much worse: he was away from God.

I took a different route. I graduated from high school with a clear calling from God. I went to Bible college. While Eric focused on partying, I prepared to become a pastor. As I grew in my walk with the Lord and in my understanding of salvation, I became even more distressed about my brother. I had tried to console myself with the thought that he had made a decision for Jesus as a child, but now I realized there was no spiritual fruit in my brother's life, no evidence that he had real faith.

Bible passages I had read before suddenly jumped off the page. Like when God, talking about his people who foolishly forsake their relationship with him, said, "Oh, my anguish, my anguish! I writhe in pain. Oh, the agony of my heart! My heart pounds within me, I cannot keep silent" (Jeremiah 4:19). And when Jesus wept over Jerusalem (Luke 19:41). And the time when Jesus "looked out over the crowds" and "his heart broke" because they were "like sheep with no shepherd" (Matthew 9:36, MSG).

That's how *I* felt! My heart was broken and in anguish because my brother had wandered away from Jesus and was now a sheep without the Good Shepherd. He was absolutely lost. I wonder if there's anything worse than being lost.

LOSING THINGS AND BEING LOST

I have a continual problem of misplacing my keys. *Misplacing* is a gentler word than *losing*. It makes me sound less irresponsible. The truth is, I would be embarrassed to know the cumulative amount of time I waste looking for lost—er, misplaced—keys.

A few years ago, PR Newswire ran an article stating that the average American spends two and a half days each year looking for lost items. "We collectively spend $2.7 billion each year replacing items."[1] Wow!

Think about it. How many socks in your drawer are missing their counterparts? How often do you have to lift the seat cushions of your couch to look for the remote control?

We lose our keys.

Our glasses.

Our wallets.

Our phones.

If you ever see a young parent with an infant, search her and you will find at least three pacifiers. Why? Because she knows those things disappear! The manufacturers make pacifiers with clips on them so you can attach them to Junior's stroller or clothes or nose. (The nose is not recommended by the manufacturer.) Anything to keep from losing those pacifiers!

Bottom line? Losing something stinks!

Twenty years ago, before I had moved to Dallas, I realized there is something worse than losing things: it's *being* lost.

I came to the Big D for a job interview. This was before GPS and smartphones. If you needed directions, you asked a friend or bought a map. (It sounds prehistoric now, like saber-toothed tigers, woolly mammoths, and Blockbuster video stores.)

At some point in my journey, I got turned around, took a wrong turn, and was absolutely lost. Not being from Texas, I didn't have anyone to ask for help. I drove around lost for *hours*. I started to imagine big old Texas vultures flying overhead. I wondered if the next time anyone heard about me would be in an episode of *Unsolved Mysteries*.

Finally, I found someone to give me directions, but I'll never forget my hours of desperation. It was miserable not knowing where I was or how to get to where I was staying.

Being lost is the worst!

You know who would agree with that? Jesus. He talked about the lost a lot. For instance, in Luke 15 he told a trilogy of parables. Jesus shared two stories about losing things and one about being lost.

Jesus's purpose on earth was to provide the solution for our wandering. He said he "came to seek and to save the lost" (19:10). He was willing to miss his Father and forgo heaven so others wouldn't have to.

Jesus would agree that being lost is the worst. In fact, the word *lost* that he used to describe those who are not in relationship with him is defined in a much stronger way in the original language of the Bible. It is actually a word that means "the state of ruination." An intensive is placed on the front of this word that carries the idea of something or someone being utterly destroyed or totally decimated.[2]

The words *perish* and *lost* in the Bible are both translated from the same word. Same word, same meaning.[3] It's the word we find in the most well-known and often-quoted verse in the Bible: "God so loved the world that he gave his one and only Son, that whoever believes in him shall not perish but have eternal life" (John 3:16).

It may not be popular or culturally relevant to describe those who don't know Jesus or are running from him as lost, but that *is* the word Jesus used to describe them. And so many of us know the feeling of being lost, whether in the larger sense of our lost souls or in the many small ways we are confused, distracted, or deceived.

But *lost* carries heavy implications in Scripture. The Bible refers to those who are not in a relationship with Jesus as

"hostile to God" (Romans 8:7)

"separated from Christ . . . having no hope" (Ephesians 2:12, ESV)

living in a "domain of darkness" (Colossians 1:13, ESV)

That sounds serious, doesn't it? God seems to be telling us that being lost is the worst.

LOST BUT PURSUED

I would like to amend that last statement. I said that being lost is the worst. But reflecting on my interview day in Dallas, when I didn't know where I was, didn't know where I was going, *and* didn't have anyone who cared or could help me, I realize there actually is something worse than being lost: it's being lost and *having no one looking for you* to help you find your way home.

My brother had gotten turned around, had taken a wrong turn, and was absolutely lost. But, fortunately, he *did* have someone seeking him. I was pursuing him, and pursuing is my specialty.

How can I make that claim? Because I have said on more than one occasion, with unfettered confidence, "Colonel Mustard, in the dining room, with the knife." Yeah, it was a guess, but c'mon, I knew I was right! So I boldly stepped back from the kitchen table, held my arms up in victory, and gloated to the thirteen- and eleven-year-old girls I had just beaten in the game Clue.

Our family loves this game. We take it with us on family vacations. We play it on holidays and sick days.

What I enjoy about Clue is the work that goes into the pursuit. To have the best chance of winning, you must pay close attention and ask the right questions. You need to take copious notes and follow the right leads. You must be aggressive and take risks.

What I love is that the game is never over until someone determines the killer, names the room in which the murder took place, and identifies the weapon.

There is no giving up.

There is no quitting.

The game does not end until the pursuit ends.

My Clue career makes it clear that I am the Michael Jordan, the LeBron James, the absolute GOAT of pursuing. (GOAT means the "greatest of all time" for all you non–sports fans out there.)

But my pursuit of my brother might tell a different story. I wanted Eric to come back to Jesus more than anything. So, one year I gave him an apologetics book for Christmas, thinking it might answer the questions he had. I don't think he ever opened it.

A couple of years later, Eric was living with his girlfriend while I was interning at the church in Dallas. My mom called me to announce that Eric and his girlfriend were going to get married. My parents were excited, and my mom really wanted me to officiate Eric's wedding. I wrestled with it. They were living together and not living for the Lord. After talking to them, I became convinced that they were both lost and that this would not be an unequally yoked couple, so I agreed to marry them—but with conditions. They would have to talk to me on the phone *and* meet with the pastor of the church whose building we would use. I thought the pastor and I could pay close attention and ask the right questions. Eric informed me that it would be a major waste of time but reluctantly agreed. I was hopeful, yet those meetings went nowhere.

Finally, the day came for the wedding. My strategy was to share the gospel in the ceremony. I knew that Eric and his bride might not even hear it, but when you are in pursuit, you must be aggressive and take risks. The day ended with the two of them officially married but without either of them any closer to faith in Jesus.

Eric and his wife ended up moving to New Orleans, having kids, and continuing their career of partying. When I had the chance—if we were alone or out on the golf course—I would try to talk to Eric about where he was spiritually. He would look at me with a bit of an eye roll and say, "Save it."

It hurt, and I questioned my pursuing skills (could my Hall of Fame Clue career be wrong?) and whether I should keep trying. But I knew this: There is no giving up. There is no quitting. The pursuit does not end until the lost are found.

THE HOUND OF HEAVEN

Francis Thompson was born in Lancashire, England, in 1859. He grew up wanting to become a writer, but his father wanted him to follow in his footsteps and become a physician. Francis felt he had no choice but to obey. He went to medical school but ended up leaving after eight years of study.[4]

He subsequently traveled to the big city of London to pursue his original dreams of becoming a poet. While a medical student, he became sick and developed an addiction to opium. In London, his addiction eventually led to poverty and homelessness. He slept on benches in parks and sold matches to stay alive. He became so despondent that he planned to commit suicide.[5]

Francis ultimately decided against taking his life and, in fact, saw his life turn around. Why? How? Jesus. He was raised in a strong Catholic family, and he returned to the faith of his youth.

He eventually wrote about what happened in the poem he's most known for, "The Hound of Heaven." He spent dozens of lines describing his flight from God, starting with

I fled Him, down the nights and down the days;
I fled Him, down the arches of the years;
I fled Him, down the labyrinthine ways
Of my own mind; and in the mist of tears.[6]

Francis continued by describing God's relentless pursuit of him. No matter how far he ran, God was always right behind. J. F. X. O'Conor wrote a commentary on the poem. He explained it like this: "The meaning is understood. As the hound follows the hare, never ceasing in its running, ever drawing nearer in the chase, with unhurrying and imperturbed pace, so does God follow the fleeing soul by His Divine grace."[7]

Thompson died at the age of forty-seven from tuberculosis, and G. K. Chesterton eulogized him. Thompson influenced writers such as J. R. R. Tolkien. The esteemed nineteenth-century preacher Charles Spurgeon was known to use the title of the poem "The Hound of Heaven" in his sermons to communicate how God pursues those he loves.

It is a perfect description. God is the divine seeker, chasing down those who are lost and overcoming them with his love.

That's why he sent Jesus. It's why Jesus taught this—that *God pursues the lost*—in each of the three parables he shared in Luke 15.

In the first parable, we read about a shepherd searching for a lost sheep. In the second, we witness a woman devotedly hunting for a lost coin. Jesus says,

> What man of you, having a hundred sheep, if he has lost one of them, does not leave the ninety-nine in the open country, and go after the one that is lost, until he finds it? . . .
>
> Or what woman, having ten silver coins, if she loses one coin, does not light a lamp and sweep the house and seek diligently until she finds it? (verses 4, 8, ESV)

I read these parables and wonder, *What is the big deal?*

With the shepherd, it's just one sheep out of a hundred!

It's a big deal because that one sheep represents one *person,* and that shepherd represents the one true God. To God, one person is worth everything, and he will search for a lost person until he finds him.

With the woman, it's just one small coin. What difference does it make? Why on earth would this woman put everything on hold until she found her lost coin?

It's a big deal because that one lost, inexpensive coin symbolizes one lost person who has infinite value to God.

In the third story of Luke 15, we meet a father desperate for a lost son.

An immature young son approached his father with an unusual request: a share of the estate now. This was bold because only at the father's death would a son receive this kind of inheritance. The request was the equivalent of the son saying to his father, "You are dead to me."

The father was heartbroken, but he allowed his son the freedom to make this choice. Without any pushback, the father handed over his son's inheritance.

This son ran to a far country where he "squandered his property" (verse 13, ESV). He wasted all his inheritance in "reckless living" (verse 13, ESV). Soon he had to hire himself out as a servant who took care of swine.

Can you imagine anything lower and more demeaning for a Jewish boy than feeding pigs? Listen to how Jesus described the state of this lost son:

> He was longing to be fed with the pods that the pigs ate, and no one gave him anything.
>
> But when he came to himself, he said, "How many of my father's hired servants have more than enough bread, but I perish here with hunger! I will arise and go to my father, and I will say to him, 'Father, I have sinned against heaven and before you. I am no longer worthy to be called your son. Treat me as one of your hired servants.'" (verses 16–19, ESV)

I've heard it said that sin is fun for a season. Have you ever wondered how long a season might be? I'm not sure. Some probably learn their lesson in a hurry. Others are more hardheaded, so it takes a bit longer.

I *am* sure that God specializes in knowing how to get our attention. He is the Hound of heaven and will never stop seeking those who are on the run. He is the loving, brokenhearted Father who is infinitely creative in finding ways to point his wandering children back in the direction of home. God pursues the lost, and he is still pursuing.

We are not told how long this son was on the run, but we do know he eventually came to his senses. What made him decide to return to his father? Perhaps it was the growling of his empty stomach, his feeling of loneliness, or his pleasant memories of growing up with his family. Whatever it was, one day he decided that he'd had enough. He was sick and tired of being sick and tired. It was time to quit running. It was time to go home.

"CELEBRATE GOOD TIMES, COME ON!"

When I teach others how to read the Bible, I encourage them to use their imaginations as they read, especially in the narrative sections. We're not always provided with details surrounding a story, so it can sometimes help to insert ourselves into the situation and imagine what it was like.

I think about this son going home. I imagine if I were in his situation, I would be having the same internal conversation. I would be ready to apologize, express my regret, and receive the punishment I deserved.

I would *not* be ready for what actually happened. Neither was this boy. Jesus said, "He arose and came to his father. But while he was still a long way off, his father saw him and felt compassion, and ran and embraced him and kissed him" (verse 20, ESV).

This could not have been the first time the father stared off into the distance, hoping that he might see his lost son returning home. I bet he repeatedly looked down the long road leading to his house and wondered, *Could this be the day?*

Then, finally, it happened. He saw the shadow of a person far down the road. He had learned to guard his emotions when he saw someone walking toward him. He had believed before, only to pay the price of heartbreak. But this day was different. This person's walk was so familiar. He knew this was his son. Something jumped in his heart. He felt compassion.

This father wasn't angry.

This father wasn't bitter.

This father didn't scheme revenge.

Instead, he ran to his son. *Ran.* The son had been running; now the father was. This type of behavior from an elderly man was regarded as undignified in biblical times. But the father cared too much for his son to be bothered by what other people may think of him.

Jesus was letting us know that respectable behavior is thrown out the window when a father sees a lost son returning home.

He ran to his son.

Threw his arms around him in a bear hug for the ages.

Kissed him.

Charles Spurgeon preached an entire message on this one verse of Scripture. He titled the sermon "Many Kisses for Returning Sinners." He said,

> See the contrast. There is the son, scarcely daring to think of embracing his father, yet his father has scarcely seen him before he has fallen on his neck. The condescension of God towards penitent sinners is very great. He seems to stoop from His throne of glory to fall upon the neck of a repentant sinner. God on the neck of a sinner! What a wonderful picture![8]

It is an incredible picture, isn't it? It is *exactly* how God feels about us when we get to the place of being sick and tired of being sick and tired and finally decide to go home to him. He welcomes us with open arms and celebrates because what was lost was found.

Remember what we're told about people who are lost? They are "hostile to God," "separated from Christ . . . having no hope," and living in a "domain of darkness." The lost have rejected the love of God, yet he pursues them in love. The lost are in a bad place, so God seeks to bring them to the place of his goodness.

He pursues them, and when he finally chases them down—when the lost are found and his wandering children come home—he celebrates with them like a team winning the Super Bowl.

Listen to how Jesus describes what takes place after the shepherd finds the one lost sheep.

When he has found it, he lays it on his shoulders, rejoicing. And when he comes home, he calls together his friends and his neighbors, saying to them, "Rejoice with me, for I have found my sheep that was lost." Just so, I tell you, there will be more joy in heaven over one sinner who repents than over ninety-nine righteous persons who need no repentance. (verses 5–7, ESV)

Check out what Jesus says happens after the woman finds her one lost coin.

When she has found it, she calls together her friends and neighbors, saying, "Rejoice with me, for I have found the coin that I had lost." Just so, I tell you, there is joy before the angels of God over one sinner who repents. (verses 9–10, ESV)

And the father after his one lost son decides to come home?

The father said to his servants, "Bring quickly the best robe, and put it on him, and put a ring on his hand, and shoes on his feet. And bring the fattened calf and kill it, and let us eat and celebrate. For this my son was dead, and is alive again; he was lost, and is found." And they began to celebrate. (verses 22–24, ESV)

In every parable, when the lost is found, a celebration ensues. The shepherd calls his friends and rejoices. The woman who finds her lost coin does the same. The father throws a party for his lost son who has come home.

The responses of the shepherd, the woman, and the father are intended to help us understand how God feels when someone who is lost is found.

The shepherd, woman, and father represent God.

The one lost sheep, coin, and son represent lost you or me. They represent our one lost neighbor, friend, family member, or coworker.

And when one lost person is found? A celebration breaks out in heaven. The heavenly Father says, "Bring the Ritz-Carlton diamond-waffle robe! Get the Gucci shoes! Throw a dry-aged prime bone-in ribeye on the grill! Crank up Kool and the Gang! Because "there's a party going on right here. . . . Celebrate good times, come on!"[9]

SEEK AND SAVE

Jesus was sent in love ("God so *loved* the world that he gave his one and only Son," John 3:16, emphasis added) "to seek and to save the lost" (Luke 19:10).

Here are two important things we need to notice about those who are lost whom Jesus is seeking out and saving.

First, even just *one* is valuable to Jesus.

We might assume that one person is not very significant. But we see Jesus connecting with the one. He traveled across a lake in a storm to free one demon-possessed man who lived in agony in a graveyard. He went into Samaria to talk to one woman who was separated from God and her community. He stopped everything to help one woman who had been bleeding for twelve years.

In the parables of Luke 15, the value of *one* jumps off the page. There were one lost sheep, one lost coin, and one lost son. Jesus doesn't just pursue the lost. He pursues the *one* who is lost.

Second, *everyone* is valuable to Jesus.

We might assume that some people have made themselves unworthy, but we see Jesus pursuing those whom others would have considered the most sinful and worthless. In fact, that's exactly what led Jesus to tell the three stories in Luke 15.

> The tax collectors and sinners were all drawing near to hear him. And the Pharisees and the scribes grumbled, saying, "This man receives sinners and eats with them." (verses 1–2, ESV)

The religious leaders just could not understand why Jesus would spend his time with such a derelict group of people. And not only did Jesus want to be around them, but they also wanted to be with him! They were the people who were most comfortable with him. Why? I think it's because he did not pass judgment on them. He did not look down on them. Jesus spoke to outsiders in a way they could understand.

He showed them love.

He showed them care.

He showed them concern.

The religious leaders despised Jesus for this. They could not believe he would pursue those who are lost and sinful. At best, he would seek after only those who were seeking after him.

Bible commentator William Barclay echoed this sentiment:

No Pharisee had ever dreamed of a God like that. A great Jewish scholar has admitted that this is the one absolutely new thing which Jesus taught about God—that he actually searched for us. A Jew might have agreed that those who came crawling home to God in self-abasement and prayed for pity might find it; but he would never have conceived of a God who went out to search for sinners.[10]

Jesus searched for sinners. He was sent in love to seek and save the lost. *Everyone* is valuable to Jesus. *One* is valuable to Jesus.

So, who is your one?

WHO IS YOUR ONE?

Jesus said in John 20:21, "As the Father has sent me, I am sending you." It's amazing! God values us so much, he believes in us so much, that he has given us the mission of Jesus! We are sent in love to seek and save the lost.

So, who is your one? We each need to ask ourselves, *Whom has God put in my life so he can pursue that person through me?*

You have someone in your life (probably a couple of some-ones) who is lost, is wandering, and needs a personal relationship with Jesus. It might be someone at your work or your school. It could be a family member. It may be someone you live next to. Have you considered the possibility that God put you in the house you live in so you could reach that person with his love?

It's time to identify your one, to start praying for that person every day, and to look for open doors for sharing your faith.

Who is your one?

My brother, Eric, was mine. I told you how he left home and left God behind. For seventeen years, he ran from God and I pursued him, but to no avail.

Eric and his wife were living in New Orleans, and our church in Dallas planted a church there. I sent the church planter, who was a buddy of mine, to visit my brother. I got a call from Eric requesting very kindly that I never again send a preacher to his house. My pursuing was unproductive, and I felt powerless. Eric was still in his season of thinking that sin was fun. He wasn't letting God get his attention yet.

Then, in February 2013, our grandfather, whom we were extremely close to, passed away. We both took it really hard. When the Saturday came for the funeral, Eric's wife did not come with him. That was the first time I realized they were having difficulties in their marriage.

That afternoon, we were sitting in the yard of our grandparents' hilltop house. As we talked, Eric said he really needed to "get back in church." That is when time stood still. I can't prove it, but I am pretty sure the world stopped for a moment when I heard those words. I had been praying for that for seventeen years! I said, "Eric, I don't know about much, but I do know about church. If you will just go to this church we planted—Vintage Church. My buddy is the pastor. Give it two times, and if you don't like it, I'll never ask you to go again."

He didn't respond, but it felt as though he listened. He drove home to New Orleans that night.

As I traveled back to Dallas the next day, I was about two hours away from home when I checked my Twitter account. (Of course, I wasn't driving at the time!) I was scrolling through my feed when I noticed that someone at Vintage Church had tweeted, "Packed house, so people have started sitting outside."[11] I clicked on the picture, and there was my brother! He was sitting outside, in a suit, in the New Orleans humidity.

I couldn't believe it! First, my brother was wearing a suit. Vintage is the most laid-back church ever, but Eric had not been to church in so long that he didn't know the dress code had changed over the years. More, I could not believe that my brother was actually there! I started to pray harder than I ever had before. I was shocked by what I was seeing and begged God to do something in my brother's heart.

A few days later, my brother called to tell me he had gone to the church. I tried to play it cool and act like I did not know. He began to open up about his marriage. His wife was thinking about leaving him. He was totally broken. I had never heard my brother talk like that. I sensed the Spirit of God leaning in and telling me to press him.

I told Eric that God was getting his attention. It was time to stop running. It was time to come home.

The next day, Eric called again. He said, "I'm doing it, Jarrett. Last night, I came back to the Lord." It was an answer to seventeen years' worth of prayers. The Hound of heaven won once again.

One of the top five moments of my life was traveling to New Orleans to preach a message to this congregation that my former church had helped start. After services that day, the entire church and my whole family watched as I baptized my brother in a baptismal tub in the back of a pickup truck.

We clapped.

We laughed.

We cried.

And we celebrated louder and with more joy than that city does during Mardi Gras. I can't swear to it, but I thought for a second that I heard the sounds of Kool and the Gang's song "Celebration" coming from heaven.

God pursued my one who was lost, and God will pursue *your* one.

Who is your one?

Is it your brother?

Is it the person you keep seeing at the gym?

Is it the other parent you often sit next to at your kid's games?

Is it the barista at the coffee shop you go to?

God is still pursuing, including that person. He wants to pursue your one *through you*.

That person is lost, and remember, being lost is the worst. Well, almost. The only thing worse is being lost and having no one looking for you to help you find your way home. Jesus gave you his mission: seek and save the lost. There is no giving up. There is no quitting. The pursuit does not end until the lost is found.

CHAPTER 5

RESTORING THE BROKEN

*Can God truly restore my life? Sometimes I think
I'm just too broken.*

You've got to love the reveal.

If you've watched a home-restoration TV show, you know what I mean. The show's hosts take a house that has seen better days, in disrepair and often dilapidated, and start restoring it. The house may be the victim of some abuse or years of neglect, but the hosts, typically a master carpenter and a home decorator, know exactly what to do. They start knocking down walls, replacing ceilings, installing new cabinets and countertops, and buffing the original hardwood floors. Soon the house has metamorphosed from a monstrosity into a masterpiece.

But the owners of the house haven't seen it yet. Their minds are still filled with thoughts of what used to be. What's happened to their house has happened beyond their watching eyes.

Which means it's time for . . . the reveal.

The owners are instructed to close their eyes as they are brought to the house. When they open their eyes, *boom*—they see what they could not see. They see the *result*. Their house has been restored to its original and intended glory. In fact, it's *better* than restored, better than it's ever been.

I will never be the beneficiary of a TV-show home renovation, but I maneuvered into the vicinity a couple of spring breaks ago.

I took my family on a pilgrimage to what many consider sacred ground: Magnolia Table and Magnolia Market at the Silos in Waco, Texas. You might know this area better as home to Chip and Joanna Gaines, hosts of *Fixer Upper,* one of HGTV's highest-rated television shows.

Magnolia has become a major tourist destination. The Silos alone receives more than thirty thousand visitors a week! In 2018 about 2.7 million people visited the city of Waco.[1] They didn't go to visit the Dr Pepper Museum downtown, tour Baylor University, or learn about what happened with cult leader David Koresh. They went to the city for one reason: Chip and Joanna Gaines!

We hyped driving the ninety minutes to the Wonderful World of Magnolia. Unfortunately, the whole experience was a major letdown.

We got to the restaurant for lunch, but no tables were available. It's called Magnolia *Table;* how can you not have a table? We were encouraged to come back for dinner. To get in, we would need to be in line at least two hours before they opened for dinner. *Two hours?!* I consider myself a foodie, but I'm not waiting that long in any line for any kind of food. I *might* wait two hours if there's two hundred dollars at the end of the line *and* an awesome dinner *and* my meal is brought to me by a mermaid riding a unicorn.

I spent the rest of the afternoon hangry, and I am not myself when I am hangry. We went to the Silos, which I had heard was like paradise but turned out to be more like Hobby Lobby.

Maybe it was just me, but the Fixer Upper–franchise reveal was not nearly as amazing as the reveals on the show. My visit was filled with groans of disappointment and tears of sadness.

I decided that I'm going to stick with watching *Fixer Upper* reruns. I eagerly anticipate the end of each episode, when Chip and Joanna show the couple their new home and give them the tour. The couple shout at first sight and let out gasps of surprise and tears of joy as they journey through their new home. I love that.

And you've got to love the reveal.

THE MASTER'S HAND

When I was growing up, my family owned a station wagon. I still remember piling into that car with my brother and sister for road trips to visit my grandparents. Seat belts? Back then, we didn't use them. We just bounced around in the backy-back.

Often we would drive through the night. Now a parent, I totally get why my dad did that. With multiple kids in the car, late evening is the only time there is ever any peace and quiet!

I remember waking up in the middle of the night one time and listening to my dad whisper something under his breath as he drove down the road. As a kid, I didn't know what he was saying. There was no music on, so he wasn't singing. I thought maybe he was praying, but as I listened closer, I could tell that it wasn't prayer, either.

Out of curiosity, I finally asked, "Why are you talking to yourself?" He reminded me that he was an English major in college and had to memorize certain poems. He never forgot the words and would recite them to help him stay awake as he drove in the middle of the night. I choose Red Bull or sunflower seeds. Dad chose poetry.

One of the favorites he quoted was "The Touch of the Master's Hand," by Myra Brooks Welch. He had it printed out and hanging on a wall in our home. It's a story of an out-of-tune violin that was thought to be worth very little.

'Twas battered and scarred, and the auctioneer
   Thought it scarcely worth his while

To waste much time on the old violin,
　　But held it up with a smile.
"What am I bidden, good folks," he cried,
　　"Who'll start the bidding for me?"
"A dollar, a dollar. Then two! Only two?
　　Two dollars, and who'll make it three?

"Three dollars, once; three dollars, twice;
　　Going for three . . ." But no,
From the room, far back, a gray-haired man
　　Came forward and picked up the bow;
Then wiping the dust from the old violin,
　　And tightening the loosened strings,
He played a melody pure and sweet,
　　As a caroling angel sings.

The music ceased, and the auctioneer,
　　With a voice that was quiet and low,
Said: "What am I bid for the old violin?"
　　And he held it up with the bow.
"A thousand dollars, and who'll make it two?
　　Two thousand! And who'll make it three?
Three thousand, once; three thousand, twice,
　　And going and gone," said he.

The people cheered, but some of them cried,
　　"We do not quite understand.
What changed its worth?" Swift came the reply:
　　"The touch of the Master's hand."
And many a man with life out of tune,
　　And battered and scarred with sin,
Is auctioned cheap to the thoughtless crowd
　　Much like the old violin.

A "mess of pottage," a glass of wine,
    A game—and he travels on.
He is "going" once, and "going" twice,
    He's "going" and almost "gone."
But the Master comes, and the foolish crowd
    Never can quite understand
The worth of a soul and the change that is wrought
    By the touch of the Master's hand.[2]

So often I feel like that battered, scarred violin. I've had things done to me. I've done things. Sometimes I wonder whether my life is such a mess and I'm so out of tune with God that I might be beyond repair. Ever feel that way? If so, there's good news. Yes, we are deeply in need of restoration. But God is a master, and his touch can restore us.

In the Bible, there was a prophet named Jeremiah. God wanted to teach him an important lesson. I don't know about you, but in school I learned best when teachers used object lessons to get their points across. Seeing the lesson not only helped keep my attention but also enabled me to understand the truth that was being communicated.

God sent Jeremiah to a potter's house for a real-life object lesson. When Jeremiah got there, he saw a potter working at his wheel (Jeremiah 18:1–3). Think Patrick Swayze in the movie *Ghost*. (Maybe not?) Jeremiah then observed,

The pot he was shaping from the clay was marred in his hands; so the potter formed it into another pot, shaping it as seemed best to him.

Then the word of the LORD came to me. He said, "Can I not do with you, Israel, as this potter does?" declares the LORD. "Like clay in the hand of the potter, so are you in my hand, Israel." (verses 4–6)

The lesson God was teaching Jeremiah was pretty simple.

The potter has power over the clay.

The potter works the clay.

The potter forms the clay.

If the clay has a lump or if it is "spoiled in the potter's hand" (verse 4, ESV) or "marred," the potter is able to rework it into another vessel as he sees fit.

WE ARE ALL BROKEN

Broken.

Spoiled.

Ruined.

This word in the Bible is also translated as "useless." It means marred or corrupted.[3]

This past summer, the air conditioner broke in our home. You haven't experienced misery until you try to sleep in a home in Texas in the middle of summer without air-conditioning. At one point, the temperature gauge in our room read 117 degrees. When the water in our toilets started boiling, I knew we were in trouble.

We called companies, got opinions, took bids, and sweat through our clothes until the air conditioner was finally fixed. An air conditioner is good only if it's fulfilling the purpose that it was created for: to cool the house. A broken air conditioner is good for nothing.

The Bible teaches that sin ruins us. To use Jeremiah's term, sin is what spoils us.

But we've all sinned. Just read the book of Romans.

What does this mean? That before Jesus, all of us were spoiled.

Before Jesus, all of us were marred.

Before Jesus, all of us were broken by our sin.

We know this. We know it from experience. We make decisions every day that lead to regret and cause pain. We have thoughts and motives that don't honor God. This is the essence of what it means to be broken. And in our broken state, there is nothing we can do to fix ourselves.

We've all tried, though, haven't we? Before we met Jesus and likely afterward too. (It takes a while for some lessons to sink in.)

We try the next relationship.

We try doing better.

We try climbing the corporate ladder.

We try more education.

Each time, we think that will be the fix.

We try bigger homes and more toys or expanding our portfolios and influence, but we are still broken. Ultimately, the only thing that can really fix us is the One who formed us! Only the potter can rework the clay.

Before Chip and Joanna Gaines ever began restoring broken, dilapidated homes, Jesus was in the business of restoring broken, dilapidated lives.

CAUGHT IN THE ACT

The goal of the religious leaders was to stop Jesus. Somehow. Someway. They were jealous of his popularity and wanted him to go away. So, they came up with a plan: entrapment.

The religious leaders were aware that Jesus loved the broken. Scripture refers to him as "a friend of tax collectors and sinners" (Matthew 11:19). His closest associates included roughneck fishermen, a political Zealot, and a hardened tax collector. He was not afraid to touch lepers, talk with prostitutes, and spend time with the questionable of society.

Judaism consisted of many laws, but committing one of the "big three" sins—idolatry, murder, and adultery—was cause for capital punishment.

Here was their plan: What if the religious leaders could catch a sinner whom Jesus loved in a sin worthy of capital punishment? If Jesus condemned the sinner, which he was obligated to do as a teacher of the Law, he would lose his reputation of compassion and empathy that so many people were attracted to. If he did not condemn the sinner, he would lose his reputation as a teacher of God's law and his credibility as the Messiah he claimed to be.

They found the perfect victim in a woman whose backstory we don't know much about. All we are told is that she "was caught in the act of adultery" (John 8:4).

There are a lot of questions we could ask. How was she caught? Where was the man she committed adultery with? Last I checked, it takes two to commit adultery. According to the Law, both parties were to be put to death for the act.

On top of this, for capital punishment to take effect, it had to be based on the evidence of two or three witnesses. That means at least two or three—maybe even four—"peeping Pharisees" had been waiting and watching for this to take place.

Everything about this smelled fishy. It looked like a setup from the very beginning and probably was.

The religious leaders brought this woman to Jesus and said, "Teacher, this woman was caught in the act of adultery. In the Law Moses commanded us to stone such women. Now what do you say?" (verses 4–5).

Bam! They had caught Jesus in an impossible situation. All eyes were on him and on this woman.

Can you imagine her shame?

Can you see how ugly and dirty she must have felt?

I wonder if she was wearing any clothes.

I envision her with a bloody lip from where one of the religious leaders backhanded her in punishment for her sin.

I see her shaking in fear with tears in her eyes.

This woman was broken. She was spoiled, and she knew she was about to die.

But then something happened. Jesus did something and then said something that saved her life. John recorded in his gospel, "Jesus bent down and started to write on the ground with his finger" (verse 6).

We can only guess what Jesus wrote on the ground. What we do know is what he said when he stood up: " 'Let any one of you who is without sin be the first to throw a stone at her.' Again he stooped down and wrote on the ground" (verses 7–8).

This is the ultimate mic drop. In one statement, Jesus forced those who were condemning the woman to examine themselves. And one by one, the religious leaders walked away until just Jesus and the woman were standing there together. Their conversation is eye opening and jaw dropping.

> Jesus straightened up and asked her, "Woman, where are they? Has no one condemned you?"
>
> "No one, sir," she said.
>
> "Then neither do I condemn you," Jesus declared. "Go now and leave your life of sin." (verses 10–11)

Just as Jesus saw straight through the religious leaders' evil plan and their deception, he saw into this woman's heart, where he perceived humility and faith.

He called her "woman"—in this instance, a term of dignity and respect. It's the same word he used to describe his mother, Mary, when he was dying on the cross. The adulterous woman called Jesus "Lord" (ESV)—a term of obedience and surrender.

As a result of her faith, she didn't get punishment.

She didn't have to pay a penance to Jesus.

She didn't receive a lecture.

Instead, Jesus offered this broken woman restoration. He offered her love, compassion, mercy, a second chance, and a new start. This is what Jesus longs to do with all those who are broken and need to be fixed.

The most beautiful part about this to me is that Jesus *wants* to fix us.

He *wants* to remake us.

He *wants* to restore us.

We are called God's "handiwork" (Ephesians 2:10). It's a word that can also be translated as "masterpiece" (NLT). Jesus wants to take our lives and shape us and form us into something special.

PLAY-DOH

Play-Doh can be easily and quickly spotted in our house full of kids. My girls know that the longer they take care of their Play-Doh, the longer it will last. When it's first taken out of the container, it's soft and pliable and will take any shape or form the girls desire.

If left out and not taken care of, though, that same Play-Doh becomes hard, brittle, and not nearly as easy to work with and shape.

Now, don't take this metaphor too far, but what's true with Play-Doh is true with our lives. If we want Jesus to restore us and remake us, help us love God and love people more, and help us become more alive in him, we have to remain soft and pliable. This happens mainly through listening to and, even more importantly, *obeying* God's Word. The writer of Hebrews puts it like this: "Today, if you hear his voice, do not harden your hearts as you did in the rebellion" (3:15).

That hardening is a picture of calloused skin. When you look at the hands of someone who works out or swings a hammer or golf club, you will see calloused skin. It is dead skin that has hardened because of constant irritation and friction. It tells you something about what the person does.

The Bible teaches that when we don't listen to and obey God's voice, our hearts harden. They become like dead skin. The harder our hearts get, the less pliable we are in the hands of the master potter.

Hardening is a slow process that takes place over a long period of time.

It happens subtly.

It can happen without our even being aware of it.

And this is exactly what Satan wants. He wants to lull us to sleep, dull our senses, and slowly and methodically lead us further and further away from God.

F IS FOR FAILURE

Peter knew what it was like for one's heart to become hard and to feel far away from God.

He was the de facto leader of the disciples. He promised that even if everyone else abandoned Jesus, he never would. Ever.

That was his promise. He was certain he could keep it.

You know what happened. Peter followed Jesus into the courtyard of Caiaphas, the high priest, to peek in on Jesus's trial. On three different occasions, he was confronted and accused of being a follower of Jesus. Each time, Peter denied Jesus, just as predicted.

We're told that as Peter denied Jesus the third time, "the Lord turned and looked at Peter. And Peter remembered the saying of the Lord, how he had said to him, 'Before the rooster crows today, you will deny me three times.' And he went out and wept bitterly" (Luke 22:61–62, ESV).

Peter failed. Big-time. Three swings. Three misses.

He must have felt like such a failure. Can you imagine locking eyes with Jesus right as you deny knowing him? Peter wept bitter tears. How could Jesus ever forgive him? How could he ever forgive himself?

Have you ever felt like you failed Jesus and couldn't imagine him ever forgiving you?

Maybe it's a divorce. It was your fault. Your actions led to the breakup of your home. Your relationship with your kids is a wreck. You feel like a failure.

Maybe it's that habitual sin you can't seem to kick. You feel so guilty for clicking on the pornography, and you promise God time after time you won't do it again. But you never can seem to keep your promise. You believe you're a failure.

Maybe there's abuse in your past. The anger and bitterness you are holding in is holding you back from moving forward in forgiveness and in your walk with God. Feelings of guilt are compounded by feelings of shame because you can't seem to let go of what happened to you. You can't seem to move past your past, so you think God sees you as a failure.

Peter could relate. He saw Jesus after his resurrection but never brought up his denial. I'm thinking Peter wanted to forget it ever happened. The only problem is that Jesus is God—and he doesn't forget!

This was the single biggest failure of Peter's life. How could he ever forget this? How could he ever forget the look on Jesus's face when their eyes met back in Caiaphas's courtyard? Peter thought he would never get over or get past this. It's a failure that would always define him.

Or would it?

GONE FISHIN'

Jesus commanded the disciples to go to Galilee and wait for him there. Galilee was the perfect place for Peter. Finally, out of the big city of Jerusalem, this was where he was most at home and comfortable.

Peter grew up in Galilee. The Sea of Galilee was where he learned to fish. It was his happy place.

We all have a happy place, don't we? For some it's a cabin in the mountains or a condo on the beach. I know friends who would rather be on a golf course than anywhere else in the world. I have other friends who would live in the woods and hunt their own food if they could. (I really pray for those friends.)

I have some friends who are like Peter. Give them a lake and some fishing gear and leave them alone. There is nothing they love more than passing the time by casting a lure and reeling it in while watching the wind blow the water in whatever direction it dictates.

I have a feeling this was Peter.

He needed to get away.

He needed the time to pass.

He needed to try to forget some things.

So, he decided to go to his happy place, the Sea of Galilee, and do some fishing. John tells us in his gospel that six other disciples decided to go with Peter. John puts it bluntly: "They went out and got into the boat, but that night they caught nothing" (John 21:3).

So much for forgetting what failure feels like! I've been fishing many times, and I can tell you that (for me at least) fishing is fun only when you are catching something. I imagine that's especially true when your livelihood depends on it.

These disciples fished all night and came up empty. They had nothing to show for their efforts except some nasty nets, stretched-thin tempers, and deflated egos. I've got to imagine that Peter was on the verge of a breakdown. He was failing at the only thing he needed to be really good at!

But then something happened. Do you remember?

A voice from the shoreline shouted, "Friends, haven't you any fish?" (verse 5).

Great, stranger. Sure, rub it in. Not only did Peter feel like a failure, but now he also had to admit it out loud. He and the other disciples had no idea it was Jesus asking the question.

From the shore, Jesus told them to cast their net on the right side of the boat. This was reminiscent of the first time Peter experienced the miracle-working power of Jesus.

The disciples did what the man on the shore suggested. What did they have to lose? John explained it this way:

> When they did, they were unable to haul the net in because of the large number of fish.
>
> Then the disciple whom Jesus loved said to Peter, "It is the Lord!" As soon as Simon Peter heard him say, "It is the Lord," he wrapped his outer garment around him (for he had taken it off) and jumped into the water. The other disciples followed in the boat, towing the net full of fish, for they were not far from shore, about a hundred yards. (verses 6–8)

Peter wanted to see Jesus.

Jesus wanted to see Peter.

There was something they needed to talk about. Peter's denial had to be dealt with. His failure had to be confronted.

When Jesus remakes us and reforms us, it may hurt a little. Like a doctor, he may have to probe and pick at the wound, but ultimately he is trying to heal it. Jesus asked Peter, "Simon son of John, do you love me more than these?" (verse 15).

Jesus wanted to know Peter's priorities. He wanted to know whether Peter loved him more than the fish he had just caught.

Jesus asked Peter the same question a second time. "Simon son of John, do you love me?" (verse 16).

The question was pointed. It was direct. In that same verse, Peter answered him directly, "Yes, Lord, you know that I love you."

Then a third time, Jesus asked the same question. One for each denial. This time it cut Peter to the heart.

"Simon son of John, do you love me?"

Peter was hurt because Jesus asked him the third time, "Do you love me?" He said, "Lord, you know all things; you know that I love you."

Jesus said, "Feed my sheep." (verse 17)

People call this passage of Scripture "The Restoration of Peter." Part of Peter's personality was his boldness, but you get a sense that now Peter was not nearly as arrogant as before.

Jesus asked him the same question three different times, pushing Peter to reaffirm his love and commitment to Jesus. In doing so, Jesus was restoring him to service in the kingdom.

He was gently remaking Peter the failure into Peter the apostle, who would preach at Pentecost and be the leader of the early church.

CALL JEFF AND CHERYL

"You need to call Jeff and Cheryl Scruggs." When I sit down with a couple and discover that they think their marriage is over, that is what I tell them. I've lost count of how many times I've said that sentence.

I first met Jeff and Cheryl in the early 2000s. They were members of our church, and their twin daughters were part of our student ministry. I was assigned to be a small-group leader at a Bible study in their home, and we immediately hit it off.

Jeff and Cheryl look like they were plucked off the streets of Hollywood. Friends refer to them as Ken and Barbie. Both are fit and successful, easygoing and fun, with a charisma that draws you in.

I came to find out that they had quite a story.

They met at a restaurant in Memphis where Cheryl worked as a waitress. Jeff walked in, immediately noticed Cheryl, and started plotting how to make his move. They started dating, and Jeff asked Cheryl to marry him nine months later.

They moved to Southern California, where both held sales-and-marketing positions at prestigious companies. With those positions came significant paychecks. They became accustomed to having the best.

An ocean-view home.

Vacations wherever they desired.

Amazing clothes.

Luxurious cars.

They had it all—even beautiful twin daughters.

Jeff and Cheryl thought they were living the perfect life. But over time, something began eating away at Cheryl. She didn't know why, but she felt like she was missing something, like she was empty, and she began getting angry at Jeff. They weren't communicating much, so Cheryl didn't tell him. Instead, she threw herself into her work. Between being good at her job and being attractive, she began to catch the attention of several co-workers. She loved it.

Cheryl's job required her to travel, and on a business trip, she and a coworker began to talk about their marriage struggles. That conversation eventually led to an affair.

Jeff was oblivious to it. He was just caught up in running a business and raising infant girls.

Cheryl decided that she was done with Jeff. She announced that the marriage was over. Jeff couldn't figure out what had happened. Cheryl wasn't giving him any answers and refused to go to counseling.

In the middle of this mess, Jeff and Cheryl relocated to Dallas.

With their marriage falling apart, they decided to go to church together. Jeff grew up in church but had walked away from his faith in college. Cheryl grew up Catholic and had avoided church as an adult. At age thirty-three, Cheryl heard the gospel for the first time. She desperately wanted what she heard but didn't want

to give up what she had. She continued in the affair and ultimately filed for divorce. Jeff was in shock.

What had happened to their life?

What was going to happen to their girls?

Why was Cheryl giving up so easily?

After the divorce was complete, Jeff became increasingly
angry at Cheryl. He would talk to her only if the subject was
their daughters.

Jeff decided to move on.

Interestingly, Cheryl was having second thoughts. Three
months after the divorce, she was continuing to attend church.
Each time she went, she would hear the gospel—again and again.

After two years of hearing the good news, Cheryl took a step
of faith and surrendered her life to Jesus.

She immediately sensed a desire to restore her marriage but
didn't think it was possible. Six months after the divorce, Cheryl
had felt led to write Jeff a letter apologizing to him for the failure
of their marriage. She invited herself over to his house and, shaking, read the letter out loud to Jeff. She asked him whether he
might be open to reconciliation. Jeff's short answer was "Absolutely not. And don't ever ask me again." Cheryl had lost his trust.
He was so angry that he had a hard time even looking at Cheryl.

Cheryl didn't give up. She continued growing in her relationship with Jesus and continued to believe God wanted to restore
their marriage. For five years, she prayed that God would change
Jeff's heart as she pursued reconciliation with him.

Five years.

Cheryl repeatedly invited Jeff over to dinner. Every time, Jeff
rejected her offer. Until one day he didn't. He finally said yes.
They began to talk again.

What Cheryl didn't know is that Jeff held on to the letter she
had read to him years before. When he didn't have the girls, he
would take the letter out, read it, and often cry himself to sleep.

Around the same time as the divorce, some friends invited Jeff to a Bible study. He began attending on a regular basis. Their marriage was still falling apart, but God was putting Jeff back together.

After seven years of being divorced, they picked up their eleven-year-old twins from summer camp and surprised them with the news, the *reveal*: they were getting remarried!

Married for ten years.

Divorced for seven years.

Remarried now for twenty-one years.

Only God.

And now? Jeff and Cheryl have a ministry called Hope Matters Marriage Ministries, through which they share their story of God restoring their broken marriage and remaking it into something beautiful.

God is still restoring and is in the fixer-upper business.

THE BIG REVEAL

I told you that the part I can't wait for in every *Fixer Upper* episode is the reveal. It's a highlight, but some even more amazing reveals are coming.

We are promised that one day Jesus will be revealed. *That's* something we should be excited about. In fact, we "eagerly wait for our Lord Jesus Christ to be revealed" (1 Corinthians 1:7), knowing that one day he will come "to be glorified in his holy people and to be marveled at among all those who have believed" (2 Thessalonians 1:10).

Man, it's going to be so good! We will "be overjoyed when his glory is revealed" (1 Peter 4:13). You've got to love the reveal!

But Jesus is not the only one who will be revealed; *you* will. That might sound strange, but it's a major theme in the Bible.[4] In fact, you know how I can't wait for the end of *Fixer Upper* to see how the house was restored? Well, there is a rather large audience who feels the same way about you. "The creation waits in eager expectation for the children of God to be revealed" (Romans 8:19).

Why? Because you and I are being restored. "The Lord—who is the Spirit—makes us more and more like him as we are changed into his glorious image" (2 Corinthians 3:18, NLT).

If you have surrendered yourself to the work of the master potter, if you are allowing him to, he *is* shaping and forming you.

Sometimes we get frustrated when the progress feels slow. We may wonder whether God is really doing something and whether we're ever going to be who we should be. But capture that thought and expose it as a lie, because your faith tells you that you can be "confident of this, that he who began a good work in you will carry it on to completion until the day of Christ Jesus" (Philippians 1:6).

The issue is that you haven't seen the finished product yet. Your mind is still filled with thoughts of what used to be. God is working, but it's from the inside out, so most of what's happening in you is happening beyond your watching eyes.

> Dear friends, we are already God's children, but he has not yet shown us what we will be like when Christ appears. But we do know that we will be like him, for we will see him as he really is. (1 John 3:2, NLT)

Hold on because it's coming.

God encourages you to "set your hope on the grace to be brought to you when Jesus Christ is revealed at his coming" (1 Peter 1:13).

On that day, you will see him for who he is.

Not only that, but you will finally see *you* for who you are.

The day is coming! What will happen? "When Christ (who is your life) appears, then you too will be revealed in glory with him" (Colossians 3:4, NET).

Jesus will be revealed for who he is, and you will be revealed—in

glory—for who you truly are, right along with him. You'll discover that you have been restored to your original and intended
glory. In fact, you'll be better than restored; you'll be better than
you've ever been.

Wow.

You've got to love the reveal.

CHAPTER 6

CALMING THE ANXIOUS

<hr>

I worry all the time. I need God to calm my anxiety.
How do I get the peace he promises?

love being on a lake.

We have several family friends who own lake houses close to the Dallas area, and it's so fun when we get invited to spend a day with them.

As a kid, I grew up going to the lake, and whether it was fishing or waterskiing, being on the lake was the best.

One of my favorite memories is getting to skip school in the seventh grade and go on a fishing trip with my dad. It "accidentally" slipped my mind that I would be missing an algebra test! Oh, well. The memories with him are much better than any algebra I can remember. (Come to think of it, I don't remember any of the algebra I learned. Actually, I don't remember what algebra is! I just know it's some kind of math with numbers and letters and that whatever kind of math it is, I have not used it since I took the class.)

I have great lake memories, but one of the scariest moments of my life happened on a lake.

It was late afternoon. We were fishing in a cove and could tell from the clouds that a storm was brewing. Fast. Before I knew what was happening, my dad had me sitting on the floor of the boat as we sped toward safety. The cove we were bound for was on the other side of the lake. By the time we were halfway to the dock, rain was pouring down and whitecaps were cresting over the boat.

I remember being scared for my life as I watched lightning flash around us. I thought we were going to die and was in an absolute panic. I'll never forget seeing the fear on my dad's face and hearing the concern in his voice as he yelled for me to stay down.

Fortunately, we made it back. It was the roughest I've ever seen a lake, and I've never forgotten it. I am still amazed at how fast the weather turned and how quickly my father moved.

That's the thing about a lake. It can be serene one minute—there's nothing more beautiful to me than seeing a sunrise or sunset on a lake with no wind blowing. The water is as smooth as glass. But then it can be rough and churning the next.

And, of course, lakes aren't the only things that can change in the blink of an eye.

Life can be a lot like a lake. One moment you're enjoying it, you might be making memories with your family, and everything is idyllic. Then something happens. You get called into the boss's office or there's a car accident or an unwanted diagnosis from a doctor, and suddenly you find yourself in an absolute panic.

You've probably seen magazine articles in which you take a quiz to determine how many anxiety-producing factors you're experiencing. And in this time when many of us do most of our reading on the internet, there's, of course, a website all about stress, at www.stress.org. You may not want to go there because, well, yeah, it will probably stress you out. It lists the following top causes of stress.[1] I bet you can identify with a few of them.

Job pressure. Many of us experience tension with coworkers and deal with unrealistic expectations from bosses. Some of us carry intense workloads. Then there's the doughnuts and birthday cakes in the break room. (The website doesn't mention work-related sugary-carb temptations, but we all know that the struggle is real!)

Media overload. We think of social media as a pleasant diversion. Think again. Studies tell us that it can cause comparison that leads to stressful jealousy.[2] Also, having twenty-four-hour access to news (of which most is negative; can't we get some cute news stories about puppies?) and alerts repeatedly dinging on our phones adds anxiety to our lives.

Health. Chronic or terminal illness creates angst. Have you noticed that even a sore back or headache can ruin your day?

Poor nutrition. Too much sugar, too many processed foods, and too much caffeine can negatively affect our moods and alter the chemical makeup of our bodies, preventing us from being able to effectively fight off stress. (And did I mention the doughnuts in the break room?)

Finances. Some people live paycheck to paycheck, barely making it. People can lose jobs and have to file for unemployment. There's the fear, and sometimes reality, of companies cutting back or reducing retirement. Emergency medical expenses can arise. Financial issues can cause relationship issues. (Been there?)

Relationships. Speaking of relationship issues, is there anything that produces more anxiety? Whether it's arguments (maybe with your roommate, your husband, or your kids about cleaning up after themselves), unhealthy conflict resolution, ongoing tension with your parents, or a divorce, relationship struggles are a major cause of anxiety.

Sleep deprivation. Not getting sufficient sleep can slow or shut down certain essential hormones in your body. Sleep deprivation can lead to memory problems, weight gain, and heart disease.[3] My guess is that you now realize you need to get more sleep so you won't be so stressed out. But trying to figure out how to get more sleep can stress you out!

Are you feeling it? There is *so* much that can stress us out and overwhelm us with anxiety.

If you're anything like me, you start thinking about the things that cause you stress, and your mind starts reeling with thoughts like these: *I have to get up now, which sounds easy but it's not. That snooze button may be the best thing ever invented, and I've got my pillow just right. But I have to get up.* When I do, I look in the mirror—not the mirror!—and realize again that I really need to lose ten pounds. *But how am I supposed to stick to my diet when I have leftover cheesecake in the fridge and people coming over for dinner this weekend? Speaking of dinner, what will I make tonight? Do I have to go shopping again? And speaking of shopping, I still have to take the kids clothes shopping because they will not stop growing. And how do I get them off their phones? Should I take the phones away or maybe put some kind of time restrictions on using them? But that would cause World War III. I don't have time for a war with my kids because I have to get that thing done at work. Work—ugh! Why does my boss expect me to take on more work but refuse to take any duties away from me? Doesn't he realize there are only so many work hours and that I am not a slave? I should just quit. Yeah. But, of course, I can't because I have to pay for my kids' braces. If my kids don't get braces, no one will marry them, and if no one will marry them, they will live with me forever. And if they live with me forever, I will forever have to think about what's for dinner tonight and buy them new clothes. Will this ever end?*

Sometimes storms come out of nowhere, but it can also seem like we are just stuck sailing through permanently rough waters.

ROCKED TO SLEEP

Thinking about my nightmare experience on the lake reminds me of a couple of stories in the Bible about Jesus being on a lake.

When we take groups from our church to Israel, one of my favorite places is the Sea of Galilee. It is a beautiful body of water that sits between two mountain ranges. I make sure that I am up every morning to catch a glimpse of the sun peeking over the horizon to start the day. I love watching the expressions on people's faces when we put them on a boat and sail to the middle of the huge lake.

Our guides leading the trip always point out that 80 percent of Jesus's ministry took place in and around the Sea of Galilee. The Sea of Galilee is the setting for two stories that I think will help us learn how we can deal with stress and anxiety in our lives.

On one occasion, Jesus got in a boat with his disciples to "go over to the other side" (Mark 4:35). While they were on their way across the sea, "a great windstorm arose, and the waves were breaking into the boat, so that the boat was already filling" (verse 37, ESV).

This was a stressful situation. Many of the disciples were fishermen and grew up around this lake. They knew how to handle a boat, and they knew what storms to take seriously. Evidently, this was one of those storms.

Mark noted it was a "great windstorm." The word translated as "great" is where we get our word *mega*.[4] The term *megastorm* sounds like something the Weather Channel might use to boost ratings. "The megastorm is coming! Are you ready?" (Insert dramatic music here.)

Bottom line? This was no ordinary storm; it was *massive.* Some Bible translators use the phrase "a furious squall." I didn't know storms could get angry, but it appears this one was. Like George Costanza from *Seinfeld* told Jerry and Kramer, "The sea was angry that day, my friends—like an old man trying to send back soup in a deli."[5]

I can imagine what this must have been like because of my experience as a child with my dad. It was scary. You begin to feel awfully small in the face of that kind of natural rage. So, I get it: the disciples were anxious about this storm. It's worth getting nervous about. And when they looked for Jesus, they found him . . . sleeping?

"Jesus was in the stern, sleeping on a cushion" (verse 38). Read that again: Jesus was *asleep.*

It's interesting to me that what was causing so much anxiety and stress for the disciples didn't affect Jesus much. He was napping while the disciples were panicking. What was rocking their world was rocking Jesus to sleep.

We can learn a lot from the disciples in this story. They did exactly as they should in a stressful situation: they went to get Jesus.

When anxiety-inducing situations and circumstances present themselves, the first thing we need to do is go to Jesus. The disciples *did* the right thing, but they *said* the wrong thing: "Teacher, don't you care if we drown?" (verse 38).

Look, I get it. Their dry sarcasm was dripping with fear. They were sailors. They knew that they needed everyone to haul ropes and try to stay above the water. All hands on deck, literally. And he's sleeping? Come on!

The disciples said exactly what they felt. What they felt is not what was wrong. Whatever our feelings are, they are legitimate. People who are prone to anxiety aren't making it up. Those stress.org issues that cause anxiety in our lives are real. (And while I'm at it, why doesn't that website have random megastorms listed as a stressor yet?)

You know what you feel.

You know what's causing you stress and how it's taxing you physically.

You are fully aware of the anxiety causing your heart to race and keeping you up at night.

The disciples were inundated with anxiety as rain poured down and waves crashed over their boat. They said exactly what they were feeling. What they were feeling was not wrong; what they *said* was.

Look again at their choice of words: "Teacher, don't you care if we drown?"

This question makes me think the disciples must have been stressed out of their minds!

First, the disciples (no matter what they were feeling) insinuated that Jesus didn't care for them. His entire life and ministry proved the opposite. He was their leader. He called them. He taught them. He loved them.

Second, they went to the extreme of claiming they were drowning. Sure, they may have felt as though they were, but it wasn't reality. Even with water crashing over the sides, the boat wasn't capsizing (at least not yet). No one had been thrown overboard.

I know the storm was intense, but I believe this is a classic example of how anxiety has a way of robbing our clarity and focus. Just like for the disciples, when storms hit our lives unexpectedly, we can do and say things that don't reflect God's whole picture for us!

We so easily forget what is real and fall prey to what we feel. I'm not discounting what you feel; your feelings are real and important. Like a light on your car dashboard, they tell you that something is going on under the hood and needs to be addressed. Your feelings are real, but they don't always reflect reality. Stressful circumstances can make our minds race and go immediately to the worst-case scenarios. You know exactly what I'm talking about, don't you?

You go to the doctor's office, and she orders a couple of tests. As you wait for the results, your mind races to the worst-case scenario and you begin to wonder what disease you will need to start fighting. Before long, you are writing a will and planning your funeral!

You may be in a dating relationship. You have a disagreement over dinner. You get dropped off after your date and then send a text to apologize. When you don't hear back from the person immediately, your mind goes to the worst-case scenario. You assume that the relationship is over and that the person you were seeing is probably already dating someone else!

I know I am guilty of imagining the worst-case scenario even with the smaller stuff—like when I see the check engine light come on in my car. I instantly become convinced that I'm going to need to take out a loan to fix the problem, and then I spiral from there.

Stress made these disciples go from trusting Jesus to thinking that he didn't care about them and was going to let them die. If we are not careful, it will cause us to make the same mistake.

This is a good time to remind you of what we have already established in previous chapters.

God *saw* their situation and need.

God *heard* their cries.

God was about to *speak*.

The disciples woke Jesus up. "He got up, rebuked the wind and said to the waves, 'Quiet! Be still!' Then the wind died down and it was completely calm" (verse 39).

With just a word, Jesus made the storm go away. Jesus made the megastorm megacalm.

He can do the same for what is causing stress and anxiety in your life. With just a word, he can make the storm that is causing rough waters in your life smooth as glass.

That sounds great, but it's not always that simple. Sometimes, instead of calming the storm immediately, he allows us to go *through* it. That's what we learn from the second story of Jesus on the lake.

ROLLING IN THE DEEP

Jesus and the disciples had a full day of ministry. Five thousand men (not even counting all the women and children) listened to Jesus teach and watched him miraculously provide a full meal for each of them with just a little boy's lunch (John 6:1–13). A first-century Happy Meal somehow fed what may have been nearly twenty thousand people.

After a long day, Jesus wanted to get away with his disciples for some much-needed rest. Matthew recorded,

> Jesus made the disciples get into the boat and go on ahead of him to the other side, while he dismissed the crowd. After he had dismissed them, he went up on a mountainside by himself to pray. Later that night, he was there alone, and the boat was already a considerable distance from land, buffeted by the waves because the wind was against it. (14:22–24)

Not again! The disciples are caught in *another* storm! Think about the disciples' day so far. They had an intense day of ministry. Stressful? *Check.*

They had to be exhausted, but instead of resting, they were fighting wind that was against them. Think that would cause a little anxiety? *Check.*

On top of this, Jesus wasn't with them this time. To make matters worse, as they struggled to battle the storm in the darkness, they looked out over the water and saw what they believed was a ghost walking toward them! "Shortly before dawn Jesus went out to them, walking on the lake. When the disciples saw him walking on the lake, they were terrified. 'It's a ghost,' they said, and cried out in fear" (verses 25–26).

Stress? *Check.*

Anxiety? *Check.*

Fear? *Check.*

This was not a good day. But it was about to get better.

> Jesus immediately said to them: "Take courage! It is I. Don't be afraid." (verse 27)

He saw.

He heard.

He spoke.

Notice what he said in the midst of the stressful situation. He spoke words of encouragement. "Take courage." It's as if Jesus was saying, "Just hold on. I'm here, and everything is going to be okay."

He spoke words of hope. "It is I." Literally translated, Jesus was saying, "I AM is here."[6] I AM is the covenant name of God. When Jesus said this, he was making it abundantly clear exactly who he was.

He spoke words of faith. "Don't be afraid."

I love that Jesus came to these disciples when the storm was roughest and the night was darkest.

What is true for the disciples is true for me and you. Don't think for a moment that God doesn't know what you are going through. Don't let Satan lie to you and lead you to believe that God doesn't care.

Jesus sees whatever is causing you stress and anxiety. He hears your prayers. He is using this book to say to you what he spoke to those disciples on the Sea of Galilee. Listen and you'll hear him speaking words of encouragement, hope, and faith.

When we read this story of Jesus walking on the water or hear someone preach about it, the emphasis is usually on Peter getting out of the boat and walking toward Jesus. I get it. Peter's walk is amazing. But what's *more* amazing to me is how this story starts. It begins with Jesus making his disciples get in the boat. Matthew wrote, "Jesus made the disciples get into the boat and go on ahead of him to the other side" (verse 22).

The word translated as "made" is an extremely strong term in the original language of the Bible. It means "to force or compel morally, as by authoritative command . . . by relentless persuasion."[7]

Think about this for a moment. Jesus *knew* a storm was coming, yet he *made* them get in the boat to go to the other side. This storm didn't take Jesus by surprise. That probably made the disciples upset. I can picture them debriefing with him later. "Wait. You knew the storm was coming? Um, where do I file a complaint? Is there some kind of HR department I can go to?" And get this: the storm you are in hasn't taken God by surprise either. In fact, he might have allowed the stressful situation so he could teach you that he would be present with you in the midst of it.

I was told by a friend one time, "It's one thing to trust God when you are in a mess. It's quite another thing to trust a God who leads you into the mess."

Whatever is causing you more stress and anxiety could be sent by God to teach you to rely on him more. Like the disciples, we can really learn what Jesus can do in a storm only if we are in a storm with him.

What he did with Peter he will do with me and you. Jesus *walks with us* through the storm.

Pastor Adrian Rogers one said about this story, "What is over your head is under His feet."[8]

I like that. Whatever is causing you stress, whatever is causing you anxiety—if Jesus's walking on water teaches us anything, it's that he is in control, and I assure you that he can calm the stress in your life. And if he doesn't? He'll walk with you through it.

SWEATIN' TO THE HOLIES

My personal physician is the renowned Dr. Ken Cooper of the Cooper Clinic in Dallas. If you don't know who he is, you need to take a moment to google him. His years of research and study led him to aggressively teach the value of physical exercise and the health benefits derived from it. He essentially coined the term *aerobics* and is known across the nation as the "father of aerobics."[9]

He is a member of my former church and has been a wonderful friend and encourager to me through the years. Every

November, I had my annual physical at his office. One of the questions he always asked was how I was managing my stress. Each year, he reminded me how important physical exercise is for helping cope with anxiety.

I have no doubt that physical exercise can help us manage our stress, and I would encourage everyone to break a sweat to be healthy physically. But the point of this book is to help you be healthy *spiritually*. Just like we can physically exercise and grow physically healthy and strong, we can also spiritually exercise and grow spiritually healthy and strong.

Richard Simmons had an old workout routine called *Sweatin' to the Oldies*. The spiritual-workout routine I want to suggest is what I call *Sweatin' to the Holies*. Do this workout every day, and God will use these exercises to help calm your anxiety and stress.

First, *put your mind on Christ*.

Your mind is a muscle. Just like other muscles in your body, it needs to be stretched and worked out to get stronger. If we do not constantly make it a priority to focus our thoughts on Christ, we will be like the disciples on the lake and lose our minds when stressful times come.

God wants us to experience the same kind of calm that the sea had after he commanded it to be still. But how does this happen? We have to set our minds on Christ. The Scripture says, "You will keep in perfect peace those whose minds are steadfast, because they trust in you" (Isaiah 26:3).

Paul wrote that we have a choice whether or not to put our minds on Christ. That decision leads to staggering consequences. "The mind governed by the flesh is death, but the mind governed by the Spirit is life and peace" (Romans 8:6).

To put our minds on Christ is to put our minds on God's Word. The more we meditate and think on Scripture, the more it will come to our aid when stress and anxiety begin to overwhelm us. I liken it to marinating chicken prior to grilling it. The longer it marinates, the juicier it gets. The longer we marinate in God's Word, the more it will come out when the pressures of life put the squeeze on us.

The greatest stress reliever in the world is to give Christ our minds and let his peace that passes all understanding (Philippians 4:7) guard our hearts and bring calm to our souls.

The second exercise is to *put your knees on the floor.*

Prayer is supernatural. When we pray, we get God's perspective and power. We draw strength from him. I love how *The Message* translates Paul's words to the believers in Philippi:

> Don't fret or worry. Instead of worrying, pray. Let petitions and praises shape your worries into prayers, letting God know your concerns. Before you know it, a sense of God's wholeness, everything coming together for good, will come and settle you down. It's wonderful what happens when Christ displaces worry at the center of your life. (verses 6–7)

Author Max Lucado wrote, "No one can pray and worry at the same time."[10]

In my previous book, *The Mountains Are Calling,* I shared my story of overcoming sexual abuse as a child. I remember the day I decided to come forward and share this secret of being abused that I had carried for nearly twelve years.

Talk about a stressful situation! I was nineteen and about to have a conversation with my parents, sharing with them that a childhood coach had abused me for three years. To say that I was anxious would be an understatement.

Before going home to tell my parents, I went to a small prayer room in my home church. I was the only one there. I lay on the floor, face to the ground, praying. Honestly, I didn't even know what to pray for. But something happened in that prayer room:

God gave me an inner strength that I didn't know was there. Actually, I don't think it was there until I prayed.

God does something when we come to him in prayer and lay our stresses and anxieties at his feet. Prayer demonstrates trust, and we get up stronger than we were when we knelt down. I love how the prophet Isaiah puts it:

> Those who hope in the LORD
>   will renew their strength.
> They will soar on wings like eagles;
>   they will run and not grow weary,
>   they will walk and not be faint. (Isaiah 40:31)

To do the *Sweatin' to the Holies* exercise routine, you put your mind on Christ, put your knees on the floor, and, in the final exercise, *put your hands in the air.*

By "putting your hands in the air," I am referring to worship. Pastor David Jeremiah wrote, "The greatest antidote to stress is worship."[11] When we raise our hands in the air, it represents surrender. When we truly worship God, we yield to his plans for our lives.

What if the stressful situation you find yourself in is what God is using to get you to fully surrender to him and his will? Looking at it that way, stress can actually be an ally in your life that brings you closer to Jesus.

It always amazes me in Scripture how much nature surrenders to Jesus.

The storm surrendered when Jesus said, "Be still" (Mark 4:39).

The great fish threw up Jonah as soon as God directed it to do so (Jonah 2:10).

All creation seems to surrender its will to God *except* his prized creation, humankind.

When are we going to learn?

We can turn stress into strength when we consistently practice the spiritual exercise of putting our hands in the air in worship and surrender.

You may be in a storm. It might feel like the waves are crashing and you could drown. But you are not alone. Jesus is with you, and he can bring peace to your troubled soul. The always God is *always working* to calm the anxious.

CHAPTER 7

ENCOURAGING THE FEARFUL

*My fears are overwhelming me. How do I keep
moving forward in the face of my fears?*

'm not much of a Star Wars fan. I actually have a word I call my
friends who are crazy about Star Wars: *nerds.*

I am not a nerd. (Except when it comes to football, I guess.
But then it's okay.)

However, I remember the hype around the sixth movie in the
series that, through the crazy Star Wars numbering, was *Star
Wars: Episode III.* This was the last movie in the series until a
whole new set of Star Wars movies came out. It was supposed to
be the movie that answered all the lingering questions. The biggest
question was, How did a sweet little kid like Anakin Sky-
walker become Darth Vader?

The answer?

Fear. Anakin had been warned of it by old master Yoda, who
told him, "Fear is the path to the dark side."[1] (Read that in your
best Yoda voice!)

If you remember, Anakin loved Queen Amidala, they got
married, and then Anakin saw a vision of her dying. The fear of
losing her became an open door for the dark Senator Palpatine.
He used Anakin's fear as the spot where he could attack Anakin's
faith in the Force. Basically, he whispered in Anakin's ear (I paraphrase), "You love Amidala. You cannot trust the Force. If you

want to save her, you must learn the tools of the dark side. I can help you get what you want. Trust in the Force is foolish. The Force cannot help you. Only the power of the dark side is strong enough to give you what you need. You do want to save her, don't you?"

From that entry point of fear, the dark emperor worked his way into Anakin's mind, and we watched as slowly Anakin turned to the dark side to become Darth Vader.

So, why would a pastor who doesn't love Star Wars and accuses Star Wars fans of being nerds bring this up? Because I wonder if there is more truth to it than we realize. Maybe fear really *is* the path to the dark side. Perhaps that's why the command God gives us more than any other in the Bible is "Do not fear."

Have you ever seen someone allow fear to be his path to the dark side?

A woman wants to meet a man who shares her faith, but, after waiting and waiting, she stops trusting that God will provide and settles for a man who doesn't believe. Over time, his influence leads her away from her love for God.

A high school student worries incessantly about what his friends think about him being a Christian. He stops bringing his Bible to school and then stops attending student ministry. Soon his commitment to Jesus is basically nonexistent.

A Christian guy believes in Jesus and makes God a priority but starts working at a new job—his dream job. The boss is demanding and often asks people to work weekends. On work trips, the boss takes the guys out to bars and strip clubs. The Christian is uncomfortable with missing church for work and with the "good old boy" outings, but he is scared to speak up. He prays but doesn't believe that God can help him in this situation. Over time, he starts thinking more like his boss and acting more like his co-workers. Eventually, there is a one-night stand, an affair, and a divorce.

Fear is the path to the dark side.

To be clear, I'm not suggesting that we can go through life without fear, but I do believe we can choose to face our fears. When fear attacks, how we respond is crucial. I might say it like this:

Facing our fear fortifies our faith.

Fleeing from fear fragments our faith.

When we face our fear, we see God at work in us, we trust him more, and it grows our faith. But when we flee from fear, we miss out on the opportunity to see what God can do, our confidence in him dies a little, and our faith is reduced.

And that's not all:

Facing our fear fortifies our faith *and makes more of God in our lives.*

Fleeing from fear fragments our faith *and makes less of God in our lives.*

When we face our fears, we realize how big God really is, we trust him more, and others see the courage he gave us, so it brings God glory. But when we flee from fear, it makes God seem smaller, we trust him less, and others don't see his greatness through us.

We really need to face our fears! How do we do that? I'm about to be honest and confess that I may not be the right person to give you that advice, but fortunately I know a good book that can help us.

FASTER THAN FEAR

I've always struggled with fear, often with some pretty crazy, imagination-on-overdrive fears.

When I was growing up, we lived on about an acre of land out in the country. Our yard backed up to a big overgrown field where I was convinced that the kids from Stephen King's *Children of the Corn* lived.

Every night, my dad would ask me to go put our outside dogs in their pen, which backed up to this field. Every. Single. Night. It never failed.

I would look out the back door at the gauntlet of terror. I didn't like the dark. I didn't like the field. I didn't like the idea of Malachai—the leader of the corn kids—trying to kidnap me. I would take off running as fast as I could, repeating my mantra, "I'm too fast for Malachai. I'm too fast for Malachai. I'm too fast for Malachai."

Another example: As a kid, I loved waterskiing. One of the ways to beat the heat in the North Louisiana summers is to head to the lake. But all the lakes have alligators in them. I would sit in the water, positioning myself to start skiing but imagining an alligator floating up next to me. Finally, I would take off, repeating my mantra, "I'm too fast for an alligator. I'm too fast for an alligator. I'm too fast for an alligator."

One more example: I grew up hunting. The best time to hunt is early in the morning or late in the evening. I can't tell you how often I made my way through the woods in the darkness, certain I was the one being hunted. The thought terrified me, even though I was holding a gun! "I'm too fast for a bobcat. I'm too fast for a bobcat. I'm too fast for a bobcat."

I'm pretty sure I could not outrun a bobcat, an alligator, or Malachai, but even still, my mantra kept me moving through the backyard, the lake, or the pitch-black woods.

I wonder what you fear and what can keep you moving forward even in the face of fear.

I'm not talking about a fear of alligators or imaginary bobcats. I mean more significant fears, the kind that attack your faith and rob you of peace.

It might be a fear of being insignificant, rejected, or lonely. You may have a fear of feeling broken forever, being forgotten by God, or finding out that he won't provide what you need.

We all struggle with fear. The real question is, How can we keep moving forward even in the face of it?

FACING FEARS

I told you that I may not be a good example of overcoming fear, but I know a good book to help us. In the Bible, we have countless stories of people who had to conquer fear.

When you think about it, just about everyone in the Bible who did just about anything for God had to face down fear to do it.

Noah had to face the fear of the unknown and build a boat when it had never rained.

Abraham had to face the fear of giving up what was most important to him.

Moses had to face the fear of confronting the most powerful man in the world.

Gideon had to face the fear of fighting a war when outnumbered by his enemies.

Esther had to face the fear of standing up for her people when no one else would.

David had to face the fear of the taunting giant, Goliath.

Daniel had to face the fear of the lions' den.

Peter had to face the fear of prison.

Stephen had to face the fear of upsetting the religious leaders.

Paul had to face the fear of loneliness.

John had to face the fear of being isolated and abandoned.

Facing their fears fortified their faith and made more of God in their lives. It allowed them to accomplish something that him glory.

There was another option, though. *Fleeing* from their fears would have fragmented their faith and made less of God in their lives.

Our enemy doesn't want God to receive glory, so his plan is to overwhelm us with fears and paralyze our faith. Satan tries to magnify what we're afraid of and minimize God so that he looks smaller than the object of our fears.

Maybe you have never been able to move past your past. It appears bigger than God. Or maybe the fear of never getting out of financial debt—not being able to make ends meet or pay off your student loans—looms larger than God. Or it might be that the doctor's diagnosis seems way bigger than God.

Satan wants to immobilize you and uses fear to do it.

Think of how differently the Bible would read if those people had chosen *not* to face their fears but instead to cower at them and allow Satan to paralyze their faith.

Instead of building the boat and saving his family, Noah perished with the rest of the world.

Abraham refused to obey God and forfeited his right to become the father of the Jewish faith.

Moses didn't lead God's people out of Egypt and slavery.

Gideon never went to war and didn't deliver Israel from her enemies.

Esther kept her faith to herself so she could keep her life, but all God's people lost theirs.

David never faced the giant and never won the hearts of the people.

Daniel didn't end up in the lions' den but did end up compromising his faith.

Peter avoided prison because he chose to obey people rather than God.

Stephen remained alive but dishonored God because he refused to speak up and speak out when given the chance.

Paul never made a missionary journey because he felt safer at home.

John never faced exile because he never pushed the envelope.

THINKING CHRISTMAS

All through the Bible, we find stories of people who were afraid, but one of the best places to find them might be one of the most unexpected: in the Christmas story.

I love Christmas. Everything about it. The lights. The decorations. The music. I also love Christmas cards and nativity scenes, which always paint a serene picture, but the reality was actually fear inducing. Not on a *Children of the Corn* level, but still pretty scary. That's why God kept giving one recurring message throughout the story: "Do not be afraid."

Can you imagine what it must have been like to be in Mary's sandals that first Christmas?

She was a teenager, and she was engaged to Joseph. Suddenly an angel appeared, telling her that she would give birth to the Messiah and name him Jesus.

Yikes.

She must have felt fear. I think that would be a natural reaction to an angel showing up and speaking.

Beyond that, she didn't understand why she had been chosen by God, how all this would go down, or if she were capable.

Not to mention, how was she supposed to explain her pregnancy to her parents? To the surrounding community? To Joseph? Talk about fear! Who was going to believe her?

Also, Mary was not married. Most girls look forward to their wedding days from the time they start playing with dolls. Weddings were an even bigger deal in the Bible's day than they are now. The wedding parties were a lot bigger and lasted longer. We may give a day or two to a wedding; they partied for a week or more.[2] I'm sure Mary was excited about hers, but those dreams seemed destroyed.

Mary now had to tell Joseph she was pregnant. He could divorce her and humiliate her publicly. What would the neighbors think? Can you imagine the Nazareth tabloids? The secrets? The whispers?

These weren't Mary's only fears.

She had the Son of God in her and was responsible for his safety, but they didn't have ob-gyns like we do. There were no six-month checkups. No measuring the stomach to see if the baby was growing and healthy. No sonograms. They didn't have fine medical facilities or modern-day medicine. It was not out of the norm for young mothers and infants to die during the childbirth process.

I can't fathom the onslaught of fear hitting Mary. It's no wonder that Gabriel's first message to her was "Do not be afraid" (Luke 1:30).

What do you do when you're afraid? Do you take out your phone to call a friend? Do you reach for a bottle, thinking that it may help take the edge off? Do you cower and back down, hoping the fear will dissipate?

Mary *faced her fears* with a commitment to trust God. She replied to the announcement of the angel, "I am the Lord's servant. . . . May your word to me be fulfilled" (verse 38).

Simple faith to combat complex fears.

Joseph was also afraid. The news of Mary's pregnancy had ruined all his plans, and he decided "to divorce her quietly" (Matthew 1:19). He was probably afraid for Mary and for his own life and reputation.

The shepherds became fearful. Those poor outcasts were in a field watching over their sheep when a multitude of angels lit up the sky and announced the birth of Jesus. The Bible says the shepherds were "filled with great fear" (Luke 2:9, ESV). I imagine so!

Mary, Joseph, and the shepherds were all afraid, and God gave each of them a message.

To Mary, an angel said, "Do not be afraid, Mary; you have

found favor with God. You will conceive and give birth to a son, and you are to call him Jesus" (1:30–31).

To Joseph: "Joseph son of David, do not be afraid to take Mary home as your wife, because what is conceived in her is from the Holy Spirit. She will give birth to a son, and you are to give him the name Jesus, because he will save his people from their sins" (Matthew 1:20–21).

To the shepherds: "Do not be afraid. I bring you good news that will cause great joy for all the people. Today in the town of David a Savior has been born to you; he is the Messiah, the Lord" (Luke 2:10–11).

In each instance, God told them not to fear. But it's not just a command. Every time, God explained *why* they could face down their fears: the birth of Jesus.

Why does Jesus's coming to the world allow us to overcome fear? Because it means this:

God is *with* us.

God is *for* us.

God is *in* us.

GOD IS WITH US

Writing about the birth of Jesus, Matthew quoted the prophet Isaiah: "'The virgin will conceive and give birth to a son, and they will call him Immanuel' (which means 'God with us')" (Matthew 1:23).

Jesus is called Immanuel because his birth means that God is *with* us. And if God is with us, why should we fear?

The times at the beginning of the New Testament were dark days for the Israelites. It had been hundreds of years since God had spoken to them. They had to wonder if maybe God had forgotten them. But this was not the first dark period for the people of Israel.

Hundreds of years earlier, the Jewish people were living in

exile in a foreign land and were subject to pagan rulers. They felt defeated and discouraged. God sent them a message through the prophet Isaiah. Listen to his words of encouragement and hope:

Do not fear, for I am with you;
do not be dismayed, for I am your God.
I will strengthen you and help you;
I will uphold you with my righteous right hand. (Isaiah 41:10)

We have no reason to fear when God is with us. The assurance of his presence may be one of the greatest promises in the Bible. As a pastor, I am often called on to preside over the funeral of someone who has passed away in our church. I always like to start the service by reading from Psalm 23: "Even though I walk through the darkest valley, I will fear no evil, for you are with me" (verse 4).

We don't need to fear because we know God is with us.

Picture a fourth grader being bullied at school. Then imagine that fourth grader becoming best friends with the biggest, toughest fifth grader at the school. Each day, they walk to and from home and school together. Is the fourth grader going to be afraid of the mean kid who used to pick on her? Not anymore. Because she now has someone with her who is bigger.

God is bigger than your fears, and he is with you.

GOD IS FOR US

It's not just that God is *with* us; it's also that he is *for* us.

Think about that—it's amazing! In fact, repeat that statement to yourself and see if it doesn't breed confidence in your life. Say very slowly, "God is for me." Now say it again but this time with emphasis: "God is *for* me."

Satan wants you to forget this truth. Remember, he wants to use fear to paralyze our faith and prevent God from receiving glory in our lives. He can accomplish this purpose by getting you to believe the lie that God is against you. He'll water the seed of this lie anytime he gets a chance.

I wonder if something has gone haywire in your life and convinced you that God is not for you.

Is it a secret sin?

Is it a broken relationship?

Is it abuse in your background?

Is it the failure of a business you tried to start?

Is it a debilitating injury or illness that keeps you from a healthy lifestyle?

What tempts you to believe that God is not for you?

Believing that lie feeds fear. As a result, people don't take risks or try new things. They don't address issues, resolve conflict, or try to develop good habits—all because of a fear of failure that has been fueled by the lie that "God is not for me."

But he *is*; God is so for you that he sent Jesus. Jesus is so for you that he put on flesh and came into the world to die on a cross for your sins. God *is* for you.

And if God is for you, it doesn't matter who is against you. Paul, thinking about the love of God in sending Jesus, wrote, "If God is for us, who can be against us?" (Romans 8:31).

God is for us. Period. No matter how much we run the other way. No matter how much we choose to sin against him. It will never change the fact that he is for us. Knowing and realizing this truth will help propel us to live by faith and face any fear that comes our way.

God is with us. God is for us. And . . .

GOD IS IN US

God is *in* us. God came in the flesh to identify with us and save us. His plan all along was to inhabit us with his presence. In the final hours with his disciples, Jesus taught them,

> I will ask the Father, and he will give you another advocate to help you and be with you forever—the Spirit of truth. The world cannot accept him, because it neither sees him nor knows him. But you know him, for he lives with you and will be in you. (John 14:16–17)

When we trust in Jesus for the forgiveness of our sins, the Spirit of truth comes to live in us. He is God in us. He empowers us to live like Jesus did.

Here are questions for you to consider:

Would you fear talking to your boss if you knew God was with you, standing right outside the door where the conversation was taking place? Really try to imagine yourself in that situation. What would it feel like?
Would you fear forgiving a person if you knew God would be right beside you as you had the conversation? How much courage would it give you to have him next to you?
Would you fear sharing your faith with your coworkers if you knew God was listening in and could give you the answer to any question they ask? Having God available like that would be a total game changer, wouldn't it?
Would you fear not being able to give up a sin if you knew God was right there to help you overcome its temptation?

Well, guess what? God has one-upped every one of these scenarios. He is closer than right beside you; he is *inside* you. Understanding that truth will help you face your fears.

God is with us.

God is for us.

God is in us.

When I was a kid and I was afraid, I would encourage myself by repeating my mantra, "I'm too fast for an alligator. I'm too fast for an alligator. I'm too fast for an alligator." It wasn't true, but even still, it worked. It allowed me to move forward in the face of fear.

We have a mantra that *is* true. When you find yourself facing fear-inducing circumstances, remind yourself of this:

God is *with* me. God is *for* me. God is *in* me.

Doing so will help you face your fear and fortify your faith and make more of God in your life.

HONEST TALK

If I wrote this chapter for no one else, I wrote it for me. If I'm not careful, I can sometimes allow fear to handcuff me.

I am a people pleaser by nature and can let the fear of man immobilize me. I don't want to disappoint anyone, so I may not always be totally truthful. I struggle with insecurity, so the fear of what people might think can sometimes alter the way I choose to do things. In fact, writing this book is an exercise in fighting my fears. I have to work extremely hard not to overthink every sentence, always wondering what people might think.

A study done years ago revealed that the number one fear of the average person is to speak in public. The number two fear is death. Jerry Seinfeld made a joke of that result, saying, "This means to the average person, if you have to be at a funeral, you would rather be in the casket than doing the eulogy."[3]

It's funny, but it's also true. I know that many people feel as though they'd rather die than speak in public. Well, it's my job. I stand up every week and preach in front of thousands of people.

I keep thinking that one week the fear will go away, but so far it hasn't.

I was twenty-nine years old when I was first asked to preach at the church that I later served as the teaching pastor. The church had a membership of more than forty thousand. The worship center seated seven thousand. There were three worship services every weekend.

I had felt called by God to preach since I was seventeen years old. In fact, I knew from the first time I led a Bible study with my friends as a senior in high school that God wanted me to preach.

So, you would think that when I received the phone call telling me I had the opportunity to preach at the church, I would be ecstatic, fired up, and ready to roll. I was. I was also scared to death.

I prayed all week that Jesus would return so I would not have to get in front of all those people. No, I am not joking.

Even in doing something that God called me to do, fear was right there beside me whispering in my ear, trying to make me cower. A great verse has helped me through the years when I hear fear's voice and feel it starting to grip my heart: "God gave us a spirit not of fear but of power and love and self-control" (2 Timothy 1:7, ESV).

This verse helped me face my fears that day. I walked up onstage, moving forward despite being scared out of my mind, and then preached the best way I knew how.

I faced my fear, it fortified my faith, and it made more of God in my life. I hate to think what I would have missed out on had I made a different decision.

You can face fear too. Why?

God is with you.

God is for you.

God is in you.

He is *always encouraging* the fearful.

CHAPTER 8

COMFORTING THE LONELY

*I feel so alone. If God is with me, I just can't feel it.
Can he do something about my loneliness?*

'll never forget the depth of loneliness I felt on my first day of school. This wasn't that "butterflies in the stomach" feeling when you walk into a room not knowing anyone. This felt more like loss, like anguished grief.

I remember wondering if life would ever be the same. Where would I go if I needed answers, and whom could I call if I needed help?

That first day of college has stayed with me a long time.

Oh, I'm sorry. Did you think I was talking about the first day of kindergarten? No way. On that day, I knew everyone before I showed up. I was confident. I walked in with my He-Man lunch box like I was master of my six-year-old universe. I knew nap time was right around the corner. I loved it.

But the day my mom and dad dropped me off at college? Different story.

My dad is my hero. I've looked up to him for as long as I can remember. My dad is extremely sensitive, very sentimental. I think he's the most tenderhearted man I've ever been around. He is also a strong man's man. He coached me in nearly every sport I played. As far as I remember, he never missed a practice, let alone a game. He modeled hard work and sacrifice. He got his university degree in English and was set to begin teaching school, but he took a job laying bricks because it provided more for our family. He laid bricks for the next forty years.

We were a blue-collar family for sure, but I never went without. In sports, if I needed a new glove or cleats, I always got them. And I'll never forget going to the bank with my dad and watching him pay for my new car. That black Chevy Beretta with maroon interior is still my favorite of all the cars I've ever owned.

Dad didn't just take me to church and drop me off; he *led* me to church. My earliest memory is of sitting in the back of our old station wagon as we drove home from church. (And yep, the station wagon was the ugly blue and brown kind—the one with wood paneling, because those were the days when people wanted cars made from as much wood as possible.) My dad would sing, "And if the devil doesn't like it, he can sit on a tack," and I would finish it off by screaming, "Ouch!"[1]

He was the first person I called when I asked Jesus to live in my heart. He helped me process and think through my decision to go into ministry. I have never had a bigger supporter or more faithful friend than my dad.

After years of getting in the station wagon to go to church, one day we got in the van to go to college. Yes, we had upgraded from the station wagon to a massive van. (I say *upgrade* with as much sarcasm as you can imagine.) I rode with my dad in the van, and my mom followed in my car. As we drove to Arkadelphia, Arkansas (yes, that's a real place), to Ouachita Baptist University (yes, that's a real college), my dad was unusually quiet. I didn't think much about it.

We arrived at the school, where we discovered that upperclassmen were waiting to empty our car and take my stuff up to my dorm room on the third floor. What I thought would take half a day took less than an hour.

We got the room situated the best we could and made a final

trip to Walmart. Mom and Dad loaded me up with the essentials—you know, like plenty of chips and a case of Mountain Dew. We then went back to the dorm room to drop everything off.

Finally, it was time for my parents to leave. I hugged Mom first and told her that I loved her. My mom is my most aggressive defender. I don't know if I've ever done anything wrong in her eyes. If my brother, Eric, and sister, Michelle, are reading this book, it's probably a good time to remind them that I'm the favorite.

Next, it was time to say goodbye to my dad. I went to hug him, and he broke. When I say *broke,* I mean he was sobbing, his shoulders shaking up and down. My dad is sensitive, but I had seen him cry only once or twice before. This caught me totally by surprise.

That's when I realized that I was saying goodbye to my best friend of eighteen years. I don't know why it didn't dawn on me until then.

I'm not sure how long the embrace lasted, but I knew that when we let go of each other, things would be different. As Mom and Dad got in the van to drive away, I stood there watching until it disappeared. Walking up to my room, I felt like I was carrying four or five heavy bags up the stairs. That's how much my heart was weighing me down.

I barely made it back to the room, where I fell onto my bed and cried.

Loneliness. I was lonely for home, for my family. I was lonely, period. But I think that most of all, I was lonely for my father.

PLAYLISTS

No one has ever called me eclectic. I'm pretty straightforward, normal, and conservative. I could eat the same thing for breakfast every day. I don't tend to watch weird indie movies. If the TV's on, I'm usually watching sports, not some obscure British comedy. I have never dyed my hair pink. I don't even own clothes that are pink! I'm not very eclectic *except* for the style of music I enjoy.

If I'm working out? It's a mix of '80s and '90s rock or a playlist I made of Lecrae's best.

If I'm at the beach? Give me a Jack Johnson playlist or Jimmy Buffett radio.

If I'm studying? I've created playlists of film scores and instrumental piano hymns.

If I'm flirting with my wife? I put on '80s Love Songs Radio! My wife can't resist it when I serenade her with Foreigner's "I've been waiting for a girl like you to come into my life."[2]

Get me on a road trip and I'm happy listening to the best of the best from any genre covering any generation.

One thing I have noticed is that every era of music has major hit songs about loneliness.[3]

In 1949, Hank Williams released his hit "I'm So Lonesome I Could Cry."

In the '60s, the king of rock and roll, Elvis Presley, sang "Are You Lonesome Tonight?"

In the '70s, it was Eric Carmen's "All by Myself."

The '80s had Whitesnake and "Here I Go Again." (Remember it? "Here I go again on my own. . . . Like a drifter, I was born to walk alone."[4])

In 1999, the Backstreet Boys sang "Show Me the Meaning of Being Lonely."

More recently, Dua Lipa had "Scared to Be Lonely" and Hunter Hayes sang "Everybody's Got Somebody but Me."

I have a hypothesis for why songs with this theme become so popular and why so many of them are still being recorded today. Are you ready for it?

It's because we have all experienced loneliness. *All* of us.

We identify with these songs. They resonate with us because regardless of our age, demographic, or background, the feeling of loneliness and isolation, which can often result in sadness and despondency, is something we are all too familiar with. It affects all of us.

CONTACTS

It affects me. People who know me would find it hard to believe that I struggle with feelings of loneliness. I'm about as extroverted as you can get. I am a high *I* on the DISC personality assessment and a seven on the Enneagram, which means I am outgoing and friendly and seek interaction with others.

For me, it's quite an accomplishment to write a book or study for a sermon because it means that I forced myself to sit down for a long period of focused time and attention. That's impressive because for it to happen, I have to be by myself.

It's impossible for me to write at the office because if I hear a conversation or someone laughing outside my door, my FOMO (fear of missing out) kicks in and I *have* to go see what's going on. I love being in the company of people and have often told others that my spiritual gift is hanging out.

But even I struggle with loneliness. I remember driving down the road one time *not* listening to music or a podcast or talking on the phone. It was just me and silence.

I didn't like it.

I kept driving for a few more minutes and an overwhelming sense of loneliness came over me like clouds rolling in on a rainy day. It was unfamiliar. I wondered if the people-person part of me had worked hard to avoid it for years and it just finally caught up to me.

Lonely? Couldn't be. Not me. I have a wife. Four incredible daughters. I just looked at my phone—I have 1,920 contacts! That's almost 2,000 people to call. How could I be lonely?

I don't know, but I do know that I'm not the only one who

feels this way. I think that to some degree everyone does. A May 2020 Gallup poll reported that 24–26 percent of Americans feel lonely,[5] making them among the loneliest people in the world.[6] A Cigna Health study in 2019 revealed that 61 percent of all Americans, especially young people, feel lonely.[7] That study surprised me. I figured that the older you get, the more prone you might be to loneliness. It turns out that both are true. The University of California San Francisco revealed research in 2012 that found that 43 percent of senior adults feel lonely on a regular basis.[8]

Loneliness affects *all* of us.

How is it affecting you?

IMAGO DEI

We are made for relationship.

This theological truth plays out in our lives every day. God *never* meant for us to be lonely, because we were created to do life in community. Let's go back to the very beginning: "God said, 'Let us make mankind in our image, in our likeness.' . . . So God created mankind in his own image, in the image of God he created them; male and female he created them" (Genesis 1:26–27).

Imago Dei means the "image of God." Genesis teaches that each of us was born in the image of God. We were created in his likeness. As a mirror reflects our image, so too humans reflect the image of God.

God is Spirit, but he is revealed in three distinct persons. This is known as the Trinity.

God the Father.

God the Son.

God the Holy Spirit.

One God in three distinct persons. You may be thinking, *Jarrett, I've heard this idea before. It's pretty confusing.* You would be right! It's a divine mystery. Why wouldn't it be confusing?

There are plenty of resources available that attempt to explain the Trinity in great detail. I've read a lot of them but have ultimately decided not to try to figure everything out about the Trinity. Instead, I embrace this divine, mysterious truth as it's taught in Scripture.

The personhood of God means that the one God in three persons can think, feel, act volitionally, and communicate. We are made in the image of God, in his likeness—not in appearance but in personhood.

God, because he is one God but exists in three distinct persons, has never been alone. Think about that. God has always had perfect fellowship with himself. God the Father, God the Son, and God the Holy Spirit have eternally been in perfect harmony and unity.

We were created in God's image, which means we were made for relationship. When we are not in relationship with him and with others, we feel lonely. Why? Because of the *imago Dei*.

Pastor and author Timothy Keller put it like this:

> Adam was not lonely because he was imperfect. Adam was lonely because he was perfect. Adam was lonely because he was like God, and therefore, since he was like God, he had to have someone to love, someone to work with, someone to talk to, someone to share with.
>
> All of our other problems—our anger, our anxiety, our fear, our cowardice—arise out of sin and our imperfections. Loneliness is the one problem you have because you're made in the image of God.[9]

We are made in the image of God and therefore are made for relationship with God and others.

Do you see why feelings of loneliness can cause so much sadness and even depression? It's because we are hardwired for relationship—for connectivity, both vertically with God and horizontally with others.

So, if we're made for it, why is relationship so stinkin' hard? And what can we do to make it happen?

GOOD COMPANY

I love how the Bible is filled with real stories of real people with real problems. There's an honesty about the humanness of the Bible's heroes that is so refreshing. It lets us know that we are not alone. Feeling alone is one thing that we are not alone in. We see people in the Bible battling loneliness.

Moses felt extremely alone on many occasions while leading the people of Israel. At one point, the Israelites were whining and complaining to Moses yet again. He was so discouraged by their lack of gratitude for how God continually provided for them that he asked God to kill him at once (Numbers 11:15).

Have you ever been so tired of feeling alone that you wondered if it would be better to not live at all? Moses did.

David did too. In the Psalms, he shared some of his highs and lows. At one point, he was feeling isolated and abandoned and wrote to God about his situation. "Do not be far from me, for trouble is near and there is no one to help" (22:11).

Have you ever faced problems and felt that no one cared? David did.

Jeremiah did too. God called him to be a prophet, preaching about the coming judgment of God. No one listened. Jeremiah was thrown into prison for a period of time and must have felt so forgotten and deserted. He became known as the "weeping prophet." No doubt many of those tears were from the loneliness he felt. He wrote, "Why did I ever come out of the womb to see trouble and sorrow and to end my days in shame?" (Jeremiah 20:18).

Have you ever cried tears of loneliness? Ever felt like there was no hope? Jeremiah did.

Elijah did too. He was another prophet of God but, unlike Jeremiah, one who achieved soaring victories for the Lord. You would assume that would give Elijah joy and enthusiastic fans, but no. After his victory, he felt defeated and was totally isolated. He sat alone in the desert and prayed, "I have had enough, LORD. . . . Take my life; I am no better than my ancestors" (1 Kings 19:4).

Have you ever had unexplainable depression and no one there to talk to? Elijah did.

We all experience debilitating loneliness. In fact, this may surprise you: Jesus did too.

I mentioned earlier our trips to the Holy Land. One of the places we go during our visits to Jerusalem is a site called the House of Caiaphas. It's the courtyard the authorities brought Jesus to on the night he was arrested. A statue in the courtyard memorializes Peter's infamous denial of Christ. It's remarkable to know that you are at the very place where Jesus was falsely accused and imprisoned for the night.

Our groups are allowed to go several floors down into a pit where it's believed criminals stayed while standing trial. It's debated whether or not Jesus actually spent the night in the specific pit we stand in, but it's moving to think about. Typically, when our group is in the pit, we read from Psalm 88, reflecting on what Jesus may have been experiencing that evening. Read these words carefully:

> I am overwhelmed with troubles
>   and my life draws near to death.
> I am counted among those who go down to the pit;
>   I am like one without strength.
> I am set apart with the dead,
>   like the slain who lie in the grave,

whom you remember no more,
    who are cut off from your care.

You have put me in the lowest pit,
    in the darkest depths.
Your wrath lies heavily on me;
    you have overwhelmed me with all your waves.
You have taken from me my closest friends
    and have made me repulsive to them.
I am confined and cannot escape;
    my eyes are dim with grief. (verses 3–9)

Jesus has felt the depths of loneliness. He cried out on the cross, "My God, my God, why have you forsaken me?" (Matthew 27:46). Jesus knows the pain and heartache that loneliness brings.

Have you ever felt like you were in a pit, forsaken by God and perhaps all the people you had counted on? Jesus has too.

In fact, Jesus came to earth so you would never have to feel lonely again.

ALONE OR LONELY?

Have you noticed that there's a difference between being alone and feeling lonely? In fact, sometimes we *need* to be alone and it can actually keep us from feeling lonely.

We call this intentional practice of being alone *solitude.* Solitude takes place when we get alone by ourselves, without distraction, for an extended time with the Lord that is quiet and reflective. Why do we get alone? So we'll realize that we're not alone.

As we spend focused time with God, we hear his voice by reading Scripture and praying. Being alone with the Lord in solitude reinforces that he really is with us and so we truly are never alone. Author and theologian Richard Foster wrote a book called

Celebration of Discipline. The very first sentence of his chapter on solitude says it all: "Jesus calls us from loneliness to solitude."[10]

Jesus modeled this for us. He would often go to a mountain by himself to pray. Repeatedly, he would break away from the crowds and even his disciples to be by himself so he could be alone *with his Father.*

Jesus would also make his disciples take a break for some extended time away from the crowds. Mark recorded that after an intense time of ministry, Jesus said, "Come with me by yourselves to a quiet place and get some rest" (6:31).

Can I point out what I hope is obvious? If Jesus made his disciples get away from the crowds so they could be with him, don't you think that he'd do the same today with you? I realize that this is difficult—you may have a job, a spouse, four kids, and a dog—well, I do—so getting alone sounds like a magic trick worthy of David Copperfield. But Jesus *is* saying to us, "Come with me by yourselves to a quiet place," and we need to figure out how to make that happen.

Jesus knows that we need rest, a break, silence, and time alone so we can understand that we are never alone.

PROMISES MADE, PROMISES KEPT

When I'm struggling with loneliness and just don't feel as though God is with me, I've found it helpful to get a journal and write down promises from the Bible about God's presence being with us. You should try it. If you aren't sure where to find those verses, just google "Bible verses, God is with us." Read them. Write them down. Reflect on them throughout the day. And pray them in the evening. This will help reinforce what you know internally to be true.

When you think about it, there is something special about a promise.

I stood at the altar of our church nearly twenty years ago and made a promise to my wife to love her and be faithful to her unto death. I was so nervous. My mouth was dry. My hands were sweating. To this day, my wife reminds me of how bad my breath was as I repeated the vows to her. I made a promise to her, and she made the same promise to me. This promise binds us together.

If I mention going to get ice cream to my youngest girls, the first response out of their mouths is "Promise?" They know that a promise locks me in.

Promises are only as good as the character of the people who make them. We've all had promises broken, but when Jesus makes a promise, you can count on him to keep it. And one of the more consistent promises he makes in Scripture is that he is always with us and will never leave us. "Never will I leave you; never will I forsake you" (Hebrews 13:5).

How awesome is that? It may sometimes be difficult to believe or feel, but Jesus promised that he is with you every moment.

And before Jesus ascended, he gave the disciples their assignment and some final encouraging words to reassure them: "Surely I am with you always, to the very end of the age" (Matthew 28:20).

It's the promise of his presence. We are never alone, so we never have to feel lonely. This is the vertical dimension of how God comforts us in our loneliness.

A PLACE FOR THE LONELY TO NOT BE ALONE

Biblical community is the horizontal dimension of how God comforts us in our loneliness.

If we are lonely, we should get alone with God and then run to his people. I kind of think of the church as insulation to loneliness.

In the winter when it gets really cold outside, the better insulated your home is, the warmer the inside will be. It can be freezing outside, but if the heater is on and the house is well insulated, you can stay warm for a long time. If your house is not insulated effectively, get ready because the heating bill will go up! It is going to cost you.

Biblical community is like insulation; the more you have, the less lonely you will feel. But if you are not well insulated, it will cost you. Have you experienced that? Perhaps you drifted from church or you moved to a new city and at first didn't have a church home. You were outside of community and you felt it, and I bet there were consequences in your life.

When we give our lives to Jesus, he does more than save us from our sins; he gives us a family. "See what great love the Father has lavished on us, that we should be called children of God! And that is what we are!" (1 John 3:1).

Next time you go to church, just look around. You may not know all the people you see, but don't make the mistake of thinking they are strangers. They're not. They are family!

Some people I know struggle with loneliness because they were abandoned by a parent early in life. I don't know of anything harder to listen to than stories of people who were neglected when they were young children. The negative effects on the psyche can last a lifetime.

When I counsel young engaged couples, I always want to know about their home lives when they were growing up. More and more, I listen to stories of divorce and the unintended consequences that come along with it. Adults in their twenties and thirties share, with tears in their eyes, their memories of what it was like to be informed by their parents about an upcoming divorce. Nearly every person I've asked can remember in detail what the moment was like, even if he was only five years old when it happened.

Many people carry the wounds with them forever and have tried everything to fill the void of loneliness that has haunted them from childhood. It's why I tell singles in our church that loneliness is not a good reason to get married. One lonely person plus one lonely person does not automatically cancel out feelings of loneliness.

Perhaps you realize that your loneliness goes all the way back to your childhood. I understand. I know it's difficult, but don't let the mistakes your parents made in the past ruin the choices you make in the future.

Remember that God has provided you with a spiritual family. If you ever feel abandoned, know that God has promised to take you in: "Though my father and mother forsake me, the LORD will receive me" (Psalm 27:10).

God is our Father. He takes us in and gives us a family. "God sets the lonely in families" (68:6). *That's* the cure to loneliness. And it gets even better. He doesn't just take us in and give us a family; he gives us a *home.*

Is there anything better than home? Home is where you can relax and enjoy yourself. Home is where you are free to open the refrigerator anytime you want and eat anything you want. Home is where you can walk around freely! You get what I'm saying. Home is home.

God gives you a spiritual home, and you don't live there alone. His home is really big, and you share it with many brothers and sisters. It's just another way that he helps bring comfort to your feelings of loneliness.

So, if you're feeling lonely, do you need to get alone with God, or run to his people? Are you missing times of solitude with your Father, or times of community with your spiritual family? How can you take advantage of what he's offered to help you overcome loneliness?

ALEXA, I'M LONELY

I have Alexa in my office. I have Siri on my phone. I can get a response out of both if I tell them I am lonely.

Alexa begins with an apology. "Sorry to hear that. Talking to a friend, listening to music, or taking a walk might help. I hope you feel better soon." I tell her, "Thanks," but she doesn't respond. I feel kinda cheated.

Siri responds, "You can always talk to me." Awesome. I take Siri up on her offer and ask what I should do about my loneliness. Her answer? "I'm afraid I don't know what you should do."

Not helpful. At all.

I recently read about the app Replika. It's popular with young adults, downloaded by more than seven million people.[11] It advertises itself as the "AI companion who cares" and states, "If you're feeling down, or anxious, or you just need someone to talk to, your Replika is here for you 24/7."[12]

All one has to do is text the AI through the app and it will respond automatically with companionship. I guess that then the loneliness people feel is supposed to just melt away.

We both know that's not happening. AI will never be able to do for us what only God can. Because, ultimately, he is the one we are lonely for and is the answer to our loneliness.

When my dad dropped me off at college, I fell onto my bed and cried. I knew I was still in relationship with my dad. I knew I could call him whenever I wanted. But even still, I couldn't see him. He was in my life, but I had this ache of loneliness because it was different now. After crying for a while, I decided I had to get off my bed, put a smile on my face, and start living my new life in college. I was lonely for my father, but I knew I would see him again soon.

Maybe you're feeling lonely. I wonder if you are lonely for God. It doesn't make total sense: You're in relationship with him, you can call him whenever you want, but you can't see him. He is in your life, but it's different from what it's supposed to be and what it will be. We are told in the Bible that God has set eternity in our hearts (Ecclesiastes 3:11). Until we are with him—*fully* with him—in eternity, we will feel an ache of loneliness because it is different from what it will be. It's sad, but I would encourage you to get off your bed, put a smile on your face, and start living your new life in Christ. You are lonely for your heavenly Father, but it's okay . . .

You will see him soon.

CHAPTER 9

HELPING THE ANGRY

~~~~~~

It's probably a sin, but I get angry—a lot.
How can God help me with my anger?

Joe Perry was a Christian . . . with an anger problem.

I first met Joe nearly twenty-five years ago when I was in college. We met through his oldest son, who was one of my best friends. After I graduated, Joe called and opened the door for me to interview as an intern in the church at which I later helped pastor.

My intern "salary" left me a little short when I wanted to buy a cheeseburger from McDonald's. There was no way I could afford to live on my own. Joe and his wife, Linda, knew this and graciously allowed me to move in with them. For more than a year, they opened their home, fed me, and allowed me to wash my clothes, all rent free.

As I got to know Joe better, I learned about his past. Joe struggled for years with a quick temper and significant anger issues. Joe was a huge man—six feet five with a booming voice—so I imagine he would have been extremely intimidating.

In college, his anger caused him to get in fistfights. When he was a young adult, people he loved had to walk on eggshells around him because they never knew what might set him off, and no one wanted to be on the receiving end of his wrath.

Perhaps the biggest issue was not that Joe had an anger problem but that he was a *Christian* with an anger problem. He knew that his anger did not reflect the God of love whom he served or the life of love that God had called him to. So, his anger was making not only other people miserable but *him* as well.

Even still, Joe excused his anger. His father had a similar problem with rage. Joe guessed that his father's father and probably generations back struggled with the same bad temper. He decided there was nothing he could do about it—that it was in his blood.

That's Joe. But what about you? If you are reading this book, chances are good that you're a Christian. I wonder if you are a Christian with an anger problem. You might believe you don't have issues with anger. That's what I thought until, well, right now.

ME, ANGRY?

I am not an angry person. Except right now. Right now, I'm angry.

I don't see myself as ever really getting angry. I have a laid-back personality. On the grace-versus-judgment scale, I lean heavily toward grace, giving people the benefit of the doubt more often than not.

So, as I wrote this chapter on anger, I tried to think of the last time I was legitimately angry and was struggling. I decided to involve my family members in the process and asked them if they could remember a time when I was angry.

It was not a good decision on my part. Immediately, they began to recount memories they have of me getting angry. Each of them couldn't wait to share a story of me losing it! And this is why I'm angry right now.

My oldest, Riley, remembered a time I got angry with her when we were swimming in our pool. She and our second daughter, Kelsey, were horsing around. Riley threw a pool basketball at Kelsey and "accidentally" hit her in the face. I'm one of those crazy parents who teach their kids to *not* throw basketballs at people's faces. Of course I was angry!

Kelsey couldn't wait to jump in and share a memory of me being mad. She recalled getting locked out of the house and, in frustration, knocking on our front door so hard that she cracked the glass in the window. Again, I'm one of those crazy parents who don't approve of their kids breaking windows with their fists. Her frustration led to my frustration, and yes, I admit that I was angry. It got worse when I found out how much it would cost to replace the broken windowpane. I was totally justified in my anger, right?

Even the eight-year-old twins liked this "game" we were playing. They were talking over each other to share about a time when Dad got mad. Landry reminded me of when I got angry at her for writing with a Sharpie on our couch. I don't remember it, but evidently my anger left a permanent mark on her, just like she had left one on our couch. Am I a crazy parent for not wanting our kids to write on our couch?

Listening to the twins, I realized how my outbursts through the years may have done more damage than I could ever imagine.

The couch-writing incident had happened maybe four years earlier. The twins were just doing what kids do: picking up markers the adults had left lying around and writing on whatever they could. I got angry, inappropriately angry, and they could still vividly remember every word of my outburst.

It made me wonder how many other times my anger has gotten the best of me. How often have I flown off the handle and then forgotten about it but it's stayed etched in my girls' memories?

In that moment with my family, I wanted more than anything to justify my behavior. I didn't. I also decided not to ask for more examples. They shared enough. It was proof that I, too, have my own share of anger issues.

You might think anger really isn't that big of a deal. You might be wrong.

A BIG DEAL?

What if I told you there is something that can ruin relationships, create division in the workplace, tear apart a church, devastate intimacy in the home, and erode trust in society? And what if I told you that Satan loves igniting this something in our hearts because it opens the door for him to go to work in our lives? When we give ourselves to this something, we play right into his hands and he is able to do what he enjoys most, which is to steal our joy, kill our peace of mind, and destroy us emotionally.

I'm not done.

I've personally seen this something cripple marriages.

I've witnessed firsthand this something keep people from moving forward in their careers.

I've counseled people whose personal growth has been stunted because they've been on the receiving end of this something.

What if I also told you that this something grieves the Holy Spirit and that Jesus said it defiles you? And what if this something is one of the biggest issues holding back the cause of Christ in our country? What if it threatens our testimony and quite possibly leads people to write off Christians more than any other something out there?

If there were a *something* like that, we would prioritize stopping that something. We would hope to destroy this destructive force, right? Well, that something *does* exist. That something is anger.

Is anger really that big of a deal? Yeah, apparently it is. Jesus put anger on the same level as murder in the Sermon on the Mount. It's a bigger deal than we think and can destroy us if we're not careful. And we need to be really careful because it turns out that we are living in an anger incubator.

THE ANGER INCUBATOR

Routine is my friend. Okay, I don't want to admit it, but routine is my *best* friend. I'm not one for surprises. Go to a fast-food restaurant with me and it doesn't take me long to order. I get the same thing *every* time. Try me.

Chick-fil-A: I'll have the number one with Coke Zero. If I'm watching my weight, then I'll just take the sandwich (no delicious waffle fries) with the Zero.

Taco Bell: That'll be one bean burrito with no onions or red sauce; add nacho cheese. (I learned in college that you've got to add nacho cheese to everything you order at the Bell. It makes everything better.)

In-N-Out: I'll take the number two, mustard grilled but with no onions, and a Diet Coke. (Why do they still not have Coke Zero?)

Routine makes me not have to think. Look in my closet and you will find a couple of pairs of jeans and a small number of long- and short-sleeve shirts ranging from solids to plaids. I switch them up from day to day, but for the most part it's the same uniform. *Every* day.

I typically wake up at the same time each day. As soon as I'm up, my routine takes over.

Coffee and a breakfast bar come first.

Bible-reading plan follows.

Then comes perusing the news.

It's the same news websites every morning. *Every* morning. I go to Fox News's web page to get the conservative viewpoint and find out why I need to be angry at the liberals that day. Then I go to CNN's web page and find out why I should be angry at the conservatives.

After those two websites come more news, some sports pages, a couple of favorite blogs, and checking in on social media, and then I'm ready to get going for the day. This is my routine *every* day.

I was working on this chapter when the title of an article in my daily news reading caught my attention. It read, "Americans are living in a big 'anger incubator.' Experts have tips for regulating our rage."[1]

Anger incubator? The term was coined by a psychology professor at the University of California, Irvine. Surveys reveal that anger has been on the rise in America for the past few years. Then civil unrest and the uncertainty of the global pandemic really pushed people over the edge.

Just scroll through your Instagram or Twitter feeds and it won't take long to see people's rage on display. You read it in the comments and see it on videos.

Tempers flaring.

People talking over one another.

Obscene gestures.

Loud screaming.

It's all there. It's everywhere! I don't have a Facebook account (because I am holy), so I use my wife's account (I'm not that holy) to check in on people from time to time. I shouldn't be shocked by what I see anymore, but I always am. So many people are really angry.

Ready for a hot-take opinion that may not be too popular? What shocks me the most is the anger I see coming from Christians. Jesus said we would be known by our love. The fruit of the Holy Spirit in our lives includes patience, kindness, gentleness, and self-control (Galatians 5:22–23). That's what should mark the lives, including the social-media lives, of followers of Jesus. But I sense so much anger in the posts and videos and comments that Christians share online.

Let me be clear: The anger I'm talking about is not the righteous indignation we see in the life of Jesus. The anger I'm talking about is from Christians who are supposed to be known for their love but are directing anger toward the very objects of God's love: other people.

Last I checked, unbelievers are going to act like unbelievers, so we should not judge or get angry at them. We should think of other Christians as our brothers and sisters, so we should not be offended by or get angry at them. Then why is there so much anger? And shouldn't it be obvious that anger has never won an argument with a fellow Christian or convinced an unbeliever to believe?

So, where does all this anger come from? More importantly, how do we resolve our anger issues?

AN INSIDE JOB

Anger is an inside job. It starts in our hearts. Solomon said, "Do not be quickly provoked in your spirit, for anger resides in the lap of fools" (Ecclesiastes 7:9).

We see that anger is a big deal. Jesus said that the evil things that come out of our hearts can defile us (Matthew 15:19–20). James told us that it can lead us to miss out on the life God is trying to lead us into (James 1:20). Where does this anger come from? Jesus said it comes "out of the heart."

This is why Solomon implored his son, "Guard your heart with all vigilance, for from it are the sources of life" (Proverbs 4:23, NET).

Vigilance is a word we don't hear much, except maybe in reference to superheroes, but it means being "ever alert." Have I mentioned that I played football back in the day? Yep. Back in the eighties, I could throw a pigskin a quarter mile. I had a coach who constantly told me to keep my head "on a swivel." He was teaching me to always be on the lookout. I had to be trained to see the entire football field as quickly as possible so I could immediately react to what was taking place in the moment.

This is what it means to guard our hearts with all vigilance. We are ever alert. Our heads are on swivels as we seek to protect our hearts from letting anger get the best of us or move us toward sin.

Have I mentioned that I still like to play football? (To quote Uncle Rico from the movie *Napoleon Dynamite,* "How much you wanna make a bet I can throw a football over them mountains?"²) Something all football teams do is watch film. All week the coaches break down their own practices on film as well as watch video of the team they are preparing to play. Watching film on the other team allows coaches to identify the team's strengths and search for its weaknesses. It allows the offensive and defensive units to prepare strategies and develop schemes that they hope will increase their chances at winning the game.

Do you know that the devil has schemes set up to destroy every believer?

> Put on the full armor of God, so that you can take your stand against the devil's schemes. (Ephesians 6:11)

Satan has watched film on you. He has studied you and crafted a strategy to bring you down. He is looking for opportunities to strike. He puts a bull's-eye target on your heart and does everything in his power to exploit and provoke you to anger. He knows the damage and carnage that can be created from a wounded heart. Your anger opens the door for him.

> Be angry and do not sin; do not let the sun go down on your anger, and give no opportunity to the devil. (4:26–27, ESV)

Satan knows what sets you off. He carries the fire starter that gets you going and understands what fuels the fire within once it starts.

Anger is an inside job. It has to be dealt with at the heart level in a healthy way, or it can lead to all sorts of harmful behavior and actions that cause dysfunction, division, and devastation, both personally and relationally.

PROVOKED TO ANGER

June Hunt, an author and counselor in the Dallas area, is best known for her ministry called Hope for the Heart. She wrote of the following four ways that Satan can move us to anger by getting to our hearts.[3]

1. Hurt

We've all been victims of someone saying or doing something harmful to us. It hurts our hearts and, if left unresolved, will eventually lead to anger.

The prophet Jonah is a good example of hurt turning to anger. As an Israelite, he hated the evil Ninevites. They didn't honor God, and Jonah wanted to see them destroyed. God called Jonah to preach a message of repentance to them, and instead of bristling at his message, they embraced it. God "relented and did not bring on them the destruction he had threatened" (Jonah 3:10).

That should have encouraged Jonah. God had just used him in a Billy Graham–type way to bring an entire nation to repentance. More than 120,000 pagans turned to God and sought forgiveness. Most preachers I know would be tweeting pictures and humble-bragging about how God used them in such a great way.

But not Jonah; he was downright angry.

To Jonah this seemed very wrong, and he became angry. He prayed to the LORD, "Isn't this what I said, LORD, when I was still at home? That is what I tried to forestall by flee-ing to Tarshish. I knew that you are a gracious and compassionate God, slow to anger and abounding in love, a God who relents from sending calamity. Now, LORD, take away my life, for it is better for me to die than to live." (4:1–3)

Jonah's hurt led to such anger that he wanted God to take him out! Anger can lead us to think irrationally and act foolishly. We really have to guard our hearts.

2. Injustice

What do you do when you feel that your rights have been violated? When justice occurs, it means that something right and equitable and fair has taken place. When there is injustice, it's the exact opposite. Satan loves when injustice is directed toward us. We take it so personally, and perhaps nothing tempts us to act out in anger more quickly and rashly.

Moses saw injustice, and it led him to an act of brutality. He was out walking when he saw an Egyptian beating a Hebrew. Moses knew that the Hebrew was "one of his own people" (Exodus 2:11). Looking around and seeing that no one was watching, Moses took justice into his own hands and killed the Egyptian. Injustice led to anger, and anger caused Moses to do something he would regret for the rest of his life.

3. Fear

Anger is called a secondary emotion, as it is typically not the first emotion we feel in a situation. We usually resort to anger to cover up a more vulnerable feeling.[4] Often our anger is rooted in fear, such as fear for our future or for someone we love. We don't like fear because it makes us feel vulnerable and out of control. We turn to anger to protect ourselves and to feel as if we have some control.

When Lazarus died, his sisters, Mary and Martha, experienced grief and fear. How did those emotions come out? Anger. Their first words to Jesus when seeing him were "Lord, if you had been here, my brother would not have died" (John 11:21, 32). Fear of the unknown spilled over into anger.

4. Frustration

Frustration occurs when we want something but it doesn't happen. At that point, it doesn't take much for our frustration to boil over into anger.

Cain is a good example of frustration turning into anger. He offered a sacrifice that was not his best, and God "did not look with favor" (Genesis 4:5) on it. This made Cain "very angry, and his face was downcast" (verse 5). He was probably frustrated with himself for making the offering, with God for refusing the offering, and with his brother for giving a better offering. "His frustration led to anger, and his anger led to the murder of his own brother."[5]

What about you? Can you identify with any of these ways that Satan attempts to provoke you to anger? If we leave doors of opportunity open to him, he'll make sure to come in and set up shop every time.

OUTLETS FOR ANGER

I've noticed a few different ways that people deal with anger. I think I've practiced each of them at one time or another.

Repressing Our Anger

We get mad. We get angry. And we stuff it down. We put it as deep inside as possible. We pretend it's not there and maybe even that it never existed. We say, "Angry? No. Not at all. Not angry here," as we continue to grind our teeth to dust. Passive-aggressive types have to be especially on guard against this.

Repressed anger turns toxic, poisonous. Poison destroys the container it resides in. With our anger, that's me and you! If we repress it, anger will turn to bitterness, and bitterness can ruin us. The writer of Hebrews warned believers to watch out "that no bitter root grows up to cause trouble and defile many" (12:15).

We know we are growing into a mature Christianity when we acknowledge that we actually have a problem. We should *not* repress our anger. We need to be honest and acknowledge it. One of my favorite cartoons as a kid was *G.I. Joe*. Every episode would conclude with the words "Knowing is half the battle." (I've committed to living my life by the wisdom of the Bible and G.I. Joe.)

If we refuse to acknowledge that we are upset and instead repress our anger, we will never be able to deal with it in a biblical way. Spiritual health and healing begin when we uncover our struggles. God heals what we reveal, not what we conceal (1 John 1:9–10). Repressing our anger is never a good option.

Rehearsing Our Anger

Have you ever been guilty of rehearsing your anger? Don't pretend you don't know what I'm talking about. This is when someone hurt you and you replay what she did over and over in your mind.

I do this, and I've found it just makes me angrier!

The more I rehearse what the person did, the more I want to take revenge. I start imagining ways I can get him back. I have a field day thinking what it would be like to confront him, humiliate him, or embarrass him.

When I do that, I'm playing right into the devil's plan. I'm giving him a foothold to go to work in my life.

Releasing Our Anger

Repressing and rehearsing are passive or passive-aggressive ways of dealing with our anger. Some of us choose a more aggressive (or we could call it aggressive-aggressive) outlet. We yell. (You might say you don't yell; you "raise your voice." Same thing.) We shoot off an impulsive email without thinking or pausing. We may slam doors, walk out, or give the silent treatment, with an evil eye thrown in to make it clear that this is not a peaceful silence.

In my experience, releasing our anger never leads to good results. It's not a healthy way for us to deal with our anger, it hurts the other person, it grieves the Holy Spirit, and it can ruin our witness.

You may be thinking, *If I shouldn't repress or rehearse my anger, if I shouldn't explode and release it on the other person, what am I supposed to do with it?* There is a fourth option. It's the best way.

Replacing Our Anger

Replacing our anger starts with dealing with it head-on. We don't cover it up, sweeping it under the rug and pretending it's not there. We don't make excuses for it, pretending it's justified and not a big deal. We also don't direct our anger toward the person we're mad at or someone else.

We deal with our anger forthrightly, with the goal of replacing it. Paul wrote, "Get rid of all bitterness, rage and anger, brawling and slander, along with every form of malice. Be kind and compassionate to one another, forgiving each other, just as in Christ God forgave you" (Ephesians 4:31–32).

Kindness and compassion? Wow. In a world of judging motives, airing opinions, and not giving people grace, Paul calls for Christians to replace their anger by exercising kindness and compassion.

But *how* do we replace our anger? We bring it to God.

In the Psalms, we see people bring their honest thoughts and emotions to him. Some of the psalms are called imprecatory psalms. To *imprecate* means "to curse." These are psalms in which people go to God with their anger.

In Psalm 109, for instance, David brought his anger to God. You probably have never heard a sermon on this one. Churches tend to stay away from Psalm 109. Why? David said some things that might make people feel uncomfortable. But psalms like this one represent an important part of David's relationship with God. We all experience anger, so bringing our anger to God should be part of all our relationships with God. We need to be honest with him about whatever we're feeling.

So, are you ready for some honesty? Look what David prayed about someone he was angry at:

Let his years be few;
　　let someone else take his position.
May his children become fatherless,
　　and his wife a widow.
May his children wander as beggars
　　and be driven from their ruined homes.
May creditors seize his entire estate,
　　and strangers take all he has earned.
Let no one be kind to him;
　　let no one pity his fatherless children.
May all his offspring die.
　　May his family name be blotted out in the next generation.
　　　　(Psalm 109:8–13, NLT)

Wow. Tell us how you really feel, bro!

David's prayer was like, "I hope he loses his job. I hope he dies. I hope his kids suffer because he dies. I hope his legacy is nothing.

I hope he has no friends. I hope his kids have no friends. I hope his kids die. I pray all this in Jesus's precious name. Amen."

That is *not* how we learned to pray. I bet your parents didn't teach you, "Sit on your knees. Okay, now fold your hands. Right! Now say this: 'Now I lay me down to sleep. I hope my enemy gets hit by a truck and his kids get eaten by wild animals.'"

We weren't taught to pray like that, but maybe we should have been, because God is the healthy place for us to take our anger. You might feel embarrassed to pray like that, but remember that God already knows how you feel.

David was angry. He came to God with his anger. As David vented to God, something interesting happened: he became vulnerable. "I am poor and needy, and my heart is full of pain" (verse 22, NLT).

As David prayed, he seemed to be realizing something that most angry people don't: often anger comes from hurt. You've probably heard the expression "Hurt people hurt people." David recognized the pain behind his rage.

David brought his anger to God, he processed it with God, and look what happened in David's heart:

I will give repeated thanks to the LORD,
    praising him to everyone.
For he stands beside the needy,
    ready to save them from those who condemn them. (verses 30–31, NLT)

As David prayed, his perspective changed and his anger was replaced with worship. We need to bring our anger to God and give him room to work so he can replace it with worship, leading to kindness, compassion, and forgiveness.

HELP!

Let's look one more time at that passage about replacing our anger: "Get rid of all bitterness, rage and anger, brawling and slander, along with every form of malice. Be kind and compassionate to one another, forgiving each other, just as in Christ God forgave you" (Ephesians 4:31–32).

We are told to replace our anger with kindness and compassion and to forgive those who hurt us. How does God help the angry? Through forgiveness. We replace anger with kindness, compassion, and *forgiveness*.

Jesus *taught* forgiveness. When the disciples wanted to learn how to pray, Jesus included forgiving in his model prayer. In fact, he taught that God's forgiveness is contingent on our forgiveness of others.

> If you forgive other people when they sin against you, your
> heavenly Father will also forgive you. But if you do not for-
> give others their sins, your Father will not forgive your sins.
> (Matthew 6:14–15)

But Jesus didn't just teach it; he *modeled* forgiveness. If anyone had a right to be angry, it was Jesus. He was betrayed, abused, mocked, and crucified. He was sinless, yet the wrath of God was poured out on him for our sins.

He had a right to be angry, but Jesus didn't spew anger from the cross. He offered forgiveness. He prayed, "Father, forgive them, for they do not know what they are doing" (Luke 23:34).

Jesus also *empowers* forgiveness. You may feel as though you are not capable of forgiving someone who hurt you. But with God's help, you can. God gives us his forgiveness, and therefore we have forgiveness to give. When we accept God's forgiveness, his Spirit comes into us and empowers us to forgive. Let's be honest: Forgiveness isn't natural. It's supernatural, which means it's possible for those who are in Christ.

> As God's chosen people, holy and dearly loved, clothe yourselves with compassion, kindness, humility, gentleness and patience. Bear with each other and forgive one another if any of you has a grievance against someone. Forgive as the Lord forgave you. (Colossians 3:12–13)

God helps us in our anger. How? One powerful word: Jesus.

And that brings me back to Joe. Remember? Joe was a Christian with an anger problem.

Joe didn't like his rage, but he found it easy to excuse because his father was also an angry man and Joe assumed that the trait ran in his family.

One night when I was living at his house during my internship, Joe told me that when he was serving in his first church, a traveling evangelist by the name of Sam Cathey came to preach. After one of the revival meetings, Joe confessed his anger problem to Sam. Joe told Sam that it was something he had always struggled with and always would—that his dad was the same way and so it was in his genes.

Joe told me, "Sam put his finger right in my face and said to me, 'Son, when you came to know Jesus, you had a blood transfusion. Your sin is not in your blood anymore.' "

Sam explained that anger starts in your heart and that dealing with it begins with recognizing you have received a heart transplant. When you give your life to Jesus, he gives his life to you. You become a new person. The old is gone; the new is here (2 Corinthians 5:17). That means you don't have to be stuck in your past or in generational sin anymore.

This was a turning point for Joe. He no longer excused his anger. He realized that because of Jesus, he had the ability to change. His anger didn't subside overnight, but God began giving him victory in this area of his life.

When Joe was tempted to blow up, he remembered who he was—that he had a new identity in Christ. If he still felt upset, he would practice replacing his anger by taking it to God. Most of all, he focused on Jesus and how Jesus forgave his sin. As he did, over time it was as though Jesus's love poured into and changed his heart.

Honestly, the whole thing was a little hard for me to believe. Not the love part—I just couldn't picture Joe as an angry man. I saw him more as a gentle giant. I lived with him and watched how he treated people, the love that would exude out of him. He set an example of godliness in so many ways, one of which was leading a ministry in our church for young boys who were growing up in single-parent homes. He would take these kids on hunting and fishing trips, teaching them life lessons on how to grow and become responsible young men. You should have seen the love, support, patience, and encouragement he showed them.

I also saw how he got up early and spent time praying and reading the Bible every morning, and it finally all came together. Joe was the way he was because of Jesus. God helped Joe in his anger in the same way he's willing to help all of us: through Jesus.

CHAPTER 10

FORGIVING THE GUILTY

Can God forgive me for anything?
If so, then why do I feel so guilty?

think I was in the seventh grade. My parents took me to the booster club fundraising event for the local high school football team. The goal was to raise money to help offset costs for the team's travel and make improvements to the field and locker room.

The best way to raise money in my hometown was to bring people together for . . . bingo. People paid to play, the money went to the team, and the bingo winners received gifts as prizes. They were raffling off some pretty good gifts:

Season tickets to home football games.

Plenty of Parkway High School Panthers paraphernalia.

Free dinner at local restaurants.

The big prize came at the end of the night. It was a huge iron barbecue grill. I personally didn't care much about the grill, but I could see that my mom and dad did. They went all in buying bingo cards, even paying for me to play. Why not? The more people playing, the more chances to win!

I had played a few games earlier in the evening and once or twice had come close to shouting a victorious "Bingo!" but I was always beaten out by some lucky kid or senior adult. I was convinced those senior-adult bingo veterans knew something I didn't.

It was the last game of the night and I had a feeling it was mine to win. One of my friends who was sitting next to me grabbed an extra bingo card to play just for fun, not even having paid to enter the game!

As the numbers and letters were called out, my odds were not looking good. With each passing announcement, my chances of winning the grill were passing me by.

Then, out of nowhere, my friend looked at me and said, "Jarrett, I've got it." The unofficial card he was playing on had bingo.

There wasn't even a minute to think. The letter and number were being repeated for a final time. The next letter and number called out could produce a new winner. I had a choice to make.

I could let it go by, or I could switch cards with my buddy and claim my grill. I could smell the burgers my dad would cook on the grill. I could see the excitement on my parents' faces when their middle child won the day. The temptation was too strong. "Bingo!" I cried out as loud as I could.

The rest is history. I left that night hoisted on my parents' shoulders like the game-winning coach of a Super Bowl. We triumphantly took the grill home.

You know what else I took home? Guilt. I knew as soon as I made the switch that what I had done was wrong. I felt so ashamed that I couldn't bring myself to tell anyone. In fact, I've never told a single person until writing it out on this page nearly thirty years later. It feels really good to finally get this weight off my chest.

I guess now is also the time to apologize to the booster club. And to my parents. Though to protect my friend's honor, I'll keep his name secret. That I don't feel guilty about at all.

ORIGINAL INTENT

Have you ever felt ashamed like I did?

It might surprise you to know that humans were not originally designed to feel shame. God created Adam and Eve and put them in the Garden of Eden. "Adam and his wife were both naked, and they felt no shame" (Genesis 2:25).

Before the Fall, humans had nothing to hide, nothing to fear, and nothing for which they had to be ashamed. Then sin entered the world. In Genesis chapter 3, Adam and Eve chose to disobey God, and it changed *everything*. Their sin had devastating consequences.

Like me with the bingo grill, Adam and Eve knew they had done something wrong. Following their decision to rebel against God,

> the eyes of both of them were opened, and they realized they were naked; so they sewed fig leaves together and made coverings for themselves.
>
> Then the man and his wife heard the sound of the LORD God as he was walking in the garden in the cool of the day, and they hid from the LORD God among the trees of the garden. (verses 7–8)

Adam and Eve sinned against God, and it led to their experiencing guilt and shame for the first time. Evidently, they didn't like that feeling. It was awkward, abnormal. They did their best to absolve it, finding a creative way to cover their nakedness and then hiding from God.

Guilt and shame just sound dirty, don't they? They are the Twin Towers Satan wants to build and fortify in our lives. They are the Enemy's modus operandi to keep us living in a state of regret and dysfunction. If he can keep us in the cycle of guilt and shame, he can render us ineffective and prevent us from experiencing the abundant life Jesus promises.

GUILT PARADIGM

This may be a good time to differentiate between guilt and shame. Though closely related, they are different.

Guilt is "the fact of having committed a breach of conduct especially violating law and involving a penalty."[1]

When we sin against God, we violate his moral law. As a result, we always experience guilt. Always.

Shame is "a painful emotion caused by consciousness of guilt, shortcoming, or impropriety."[2]

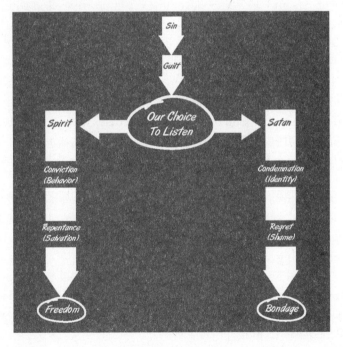

Someone can have guilt and not feel shame. It's impossible, though, to feel shame and not have a sense of guilt.

I created something that might help, which I call the guilt paradigm:

Let's walk through this. When we rebel against God, we sin.

With sin comes guilt. Guilt weighs heavily on the soul. Adam and Eve didn't like the guilt that followed their disobedience to God. They knew they had crossed a line and innately wanted their guilt absolved. God wired us that way for a purpose.

Adam and Eve tried to resolve their guilt by sewing fig leaves together to make undergarments and then attempting a game of hide-and-seek with God.

We're a bit more sophisticated in trying to pardon our guilt. At least we *think* we are.

We don't sew fig leaves together to try to exonerate our guilt; we pledge to "do better next time." We promise God that we won't do it again and that we'll go to church next week. We think this will for sure absolve our guilt.

We know we can't hide from God physically, but we *do* try to hide from him. We hide behind our busyness. It's like if we don't think about him, maybe he won't think about us. Or we hide behind some kind of substance or activity. If we drink enough wine, watch enough Netflix, eat enough ice cream, or read enough fiction, it can help deaden the sense of guilt we have over our sin.

Here's what I want you to understand: guilt is a *good thing*. God wired us to feel guilty when we disobey him. If we didn't have guilt, we would just get stuck in our sin. Don't ignore that guilty feeling.

The real battle begins when we experience that guilt. As the chart indicates, it's at that point that we have a choice. The Holy Spirit wants to bring conviction with our guilt, while Satan wants to condemn us in it.

VOICES

The Holy Spirit brings conviction of sin into our lives. Jesus said it like this:

> I tell you the truth: it is to your advantage that I go away, for if I do not go away, the Helper will not come to you. But if I go, I will send him to you. And when he comes, he will convict the world concerning sin and righteousness and judgment. (John 16:7–8, ESV)

Conviction is from God. It is always directed toward a defined wrongdoing. We feel guilty about a specific act of sin.

Condemnation is different. It's from Satan. One of his names in Scripture is "the accuser of our brothers and sisters" (Revelation 12:10). Condemnation does not mean feeling bad about a specific sin but instead is a vague sense that we are bad. The Holy Spirit convicts us for specific behavior. Satan condemns us for who we are. He attacks our identity as children of God.

I'll show you the difference using another personal illustration. (You're about to find out that not only am I a deceitful cheater in bingo but I also occasionally lie to my friends.)

A few years ago, one of my friends asked me to play basketball after work. I didn't want to play, but instead of being honest, I fudged the truth. You know, I told him how much work I had to do and how I had to go home right after work and so there was just no way I could play ball that afternoon.

Immediately, I could sense conviction in my heart. I knew better than to lie. My sin brought guilt. The Holy Spirit was, in his own gentle way, revealing to me that I had not been honest. I had lied to my friend. The conviction of the Holy Spirit is always aimed at specific behavior.

At the same time, condemnation came at me from Satan. How did I know it was condemnation from the Enemy? Because he attacked my identity as a child of God. His voice was not gentle or loving like the Holy Spirit's. Instead, it was accusatory in tone.

How could you?

I can't believe you just did that! And you call yourself a Christian?

The voice of Satan is always harsh, always condemning, and always aimed at attacking our identity as children of God.

Isn't it amazing how the Enemy lures us to sin against God and then condemns us for following his voice? Such are the ways of the devil. I've heard his whispering voice so many times through the years. Maybe you have too.

There's no way God will forgive you for doing that.
All these years and you still can't beat that sin.
You are worthless.
You are hopeless.
You are so dirty and disgusting.
You must be such a disappointment to God.

Do you see the difference between the Holy Spirit's voice of conviction and Satan's voice of condemnation?

At this point, we have a crucial choice to make. Will we listen and adhere to the voice of the Holy Spirit or the voice of the Enemy?

The stakes couldn't be higher. As you can see in my chart, one choice leads to repentance and salvation, resulting in freedom; the other leads to regret and shame, resulting in bondage.

THE CROSSROADS

After lying to my friend, I sensed conviction from the Holy Spirit *and* condemnation from Satan. I was at a crossroads. I had a decision to make.

By God's grace, I made the choice to listen to the voice of the Holy Spirit. I went to my friend, confessed that I hadn't been honest with him, and apologized for lying. My friend was gracious. He told me I was dumb for lying and even dumber for feeling like

I had to confess it to him. He was being a good friend, but I thought he was wrong. In this case, was it a big deal on the surface? No. But I sensed that I should confess it.

As believers, when we sin against God, we experience guilt. We feel conviction. When we choose to listen to the Holy Spirit's voice and lean into that conviction, he will always lead us to *repentance*. "Godly sorrow brings repentance that leads to salvation and leaves no regret" (2 Corinthians 7:10).

Making the choice to repent is proof of salvation in our lives. Choosing to cooperate with the work of the Holy Spirit in this way invites God in to make us more and more like Jesus. We see the benefits of confession and repentance as they lead us to *freedom*.

After having confessed lying to my friend, I felt free. I no longer had a secret I was hiding. I didn't have to worry about whether he might find out. I didn't have guilt hanging over me. I felt clean.

Have you experienced that? Do you know the freedom of confession and repentance? Would you agree with me that there may be no better feeling?

Conversely, if we listen to the voice of Satan, we will always end up living in regret and shame. Sadly, this is the air so many believers are breathing today.

Satan's voice is loud and penetrating. It's hard to ignore. When we sin against God, especially when it's willful disobedience against him, it's easier to listen to Satan's voice of condemnation. He is speaking what we are feeling. We may listen to his voice because we feel like it's penance for committing the sin in the first place.

The longer we listen to his condemning voice, the further we drown in the sea of regret and shame. This is extremely dangerous territory because living in shame will always lead to bondage.

Often we will stay stuck in a self-destructive cycle of repeating the same hated sin, perhaps not realizing that confession and repentance are the way out. We have thoughts like *What would happen if someone really knew me?* I've known people with such a deep amount of shame and regret that they try to dismiss what caused it by drinking themselves into forgetfulness. Others turn into perfectionists, convinced they'd never be accepted if they weren't. I've seen others who, believing they are worthless, isolate themselves, thinking that avoiding others is the easiest way not to be rejected.

We try to do what Adam and Eve did. We hide from the guilt and shame. We hide from God, fearing that we will one day be exposed. Living this way leads only to increased bondage and keeps us spinning through the cycle of shame and regret. *Cycle* is a good word to describe living in shame and guilt. It feels like you are in a wash cycle that never stops.

THREE CHOICES

Look back one more time at the guilt paradigm.

I'm sure you want to live in repentance and salvation, as that is the only way to freedom. But how can we ensure we live that way? We have to make three choices every day.

Choose the Gospel over Guilt

God made a way for guilt to be absolved. It's called the gospel.

God's been leading us to the gospel since before it was even the gospel. Back in Old Testament times, God designed a sacrificial system that beautifully foreshadowed what Jesus would one day fulfill through dying on the cross.

The holiest day of the year for the Jewish people was known as the Day of Atonement. On that special day, the high priest took blood from unblemished goats into the Most Holy Place, sprinkling it on the altar. This was known as *propitiation.* The blood of the unblemished goat appeased the wrath of God that was warranted because of the people's sin (Leviticus 16:9, 15–19).

On the second goat, the high priest confessed the sins of the people, but instead of slaughtering it, he sent it into the wilderness. This scapegoat symbolized the sins of the people being carried away (verses 20–22). This was known as *expiation*. Both sin and guilt were atoned for and carried away on the Day of Atonement.

When John the Baptist saw Jesus walking beside the Sea of Galilee, he said, "Look, the Lamb of God, who takes away the sin of the world!" (John 1:29).

In the sacrifice of Jesus, we have both propitiation and expiation. On the cross, he appeased the wrath of God *and* carried our sin away to be remembered no more. This is the gospel, and the gospel is God's answer to sin and guilt.

Three days after his sacrifice, Jesus rose from the dead. The Resurrection is so powerful because it was God declaring his acceptance of Jesus's sacrifice, demonstrating that sin and guilt had been dealt with forever.

When we sin, we must choose the gospel over guilt.

Choose Confession over Concealment

Our secrets strangle and suffocate us spiritually. We need to confess our sin. Remember, God sees everything, so we can't really hide our sin from him. Confession is simply agreeing with God that what we did was wrong.

David tried to hide his sin from God, and it had a negative effect on his life spiritually, physically, and emotionally. He wrote about it in Psalm 32:

> Blessed is the one
> whose transgressions are forgiven,
> whose sins are covered.

Blessed is the one
    whose sin the LORD does not count against them
    and in whose spirit is no deceit.

When I kept silent,
    my bones wasted away
    through my groaning all day long.
For day and night
    your hand was heavy on me;
my strength was sapped
    as in the heat of summer.

Then I acknowledged my sin to you
    and did not cover up my iniquity.
I said, "I will confess
    my transgressions to the LORD."
And you forgave
    the guilt of my sin. (verses 1–5)

When we conceal our sin, we only hurt ourselves. David was in pain. His sin was making him sick. He started feeling better only when he decided to confess his sin instead of covering it up.

Satan wants us to keep our sin in the dark because then guilt and shame can retain their grip on our lives. Satan knows that every time we confess our sin, we experience more freedom. What the darkness of our sin needs is exposure to the light. The light comes when we confess to God and other Christians. James wrote, "Confess your sins to each other and pray for each other so that you may be healed. The prayer of a righteous person is powerful and effective" (5:16).

Confession is good for the soul. It brings healing spiritually and, as James suggests, sometimes physically. If we are faithful to confess our sins, Jesus is faithful to forgive. "If we confess our sins, he is faithful and just and will forgive us our sins and purify us from all unrighteousness" (1 John 1:9).

Jesus stands ready to forgive, and when he does, he forgives *quickly*. He doesn't hold out until we make up for our sin. He forgives as soon as we confess.

To be clear, all of our sin—past, present, and future, confessed and unconfessed—was put on Jesus on the cross. He paid the price for our sin "once for all" (Hebrews 10:10). Unconfessed sin does not remove us from our relationship with God any more than my children's disobedience removes them from their relationship with me.

The forgiveness God extends when we confess our sins restores our *fellowship* with him, not our relationship. What was broken was not our relationship with God but our intimacy with him.

Also, when Jesus forgives, he forgives *completely*. There is no partial forgiveness. Jesus's blood covers *all* our sin. The psalmist wrote, "As far as the east is from the west, so far has he removed our transgressions from us" (103:12).

Isn't it good to know that Jesus isn't holding out on us? He forgives totally and completely. You may think this sounds too good to be true. If so, you *really* need to make this next choice.

Choose Facts over Feelings

Have you noticed that feelings come and go? More importantly, have you noticed that feelings can deceive you?

I love to eat. I feel like I am always hungry. If I eat every time I *feel* hungry, I will be extremely unhealthy and overweight. My feelings deceive me, and I can't live off them when it comes to my diet.

I also can't live off my feelings when it comes to dealing with shame. When we sin against God, we may *feel* condemned. Even after confessing our sin, we may still feel condemned. Our feelings deceive us. We have to live off the truth God gives us in the Bible. The Bible says, "There is now no condemnation for those who are in Christ Jesus" (Romans 8:1).

Satan wants us to believe that God can't and won't forgive us. He whispers condemning lies into our hearts. If we are not careful, our feelings will follow. We have to choose facts over feelings.

This is one truth I share with people over and over again because it's so important to our discipleship and growth as believers. I tell people that, yes, their feelings are valid and important but that it's not always wise to trust our feelings. We need to base our lives on the truth of God's Word.

TWO EXAMPLES

Let's look quickly at the lives of Peter and Judas. One is a good example of someone who made these three choices; the other is not.

Both sinned against God. Peter denied Jesus. Judas betrayed him.

Both experienced guilt. Peter wept over his denial. Judas tried to return the money he was paid for turning Jesus over to the authorities.

Here is where their paths differ.

Peter walked in *conviction*. He continued to spend time with the other disciples and was there when the news first came that Jesus had risen from the dead. He went back to Galilee, where Jesus met him on the side of the lake one morning and gently restored him. Peter repented and walked in salvation.

Peter chose the gospel over guilt.

Confession over concealment.

Facts over feelings.

Judas did just the opposite. He wallowed in guilt and was

crushed by feelings of *condemnation.* He felt so condemned that he took his own life.

That is what guilt and shame will do. They will overwhelm you and take your life. We were not created to walk in shame. It can be different. Your life *can* change.

Just take a step. Make the choice. Choose to listen to God's voice as he convicts you. Is there a sin for which you need to confess and repent? God is always forgiving the guilty, and he can set you free today.

ALWAYS
FAITHFUL

CHAPTER 11

TRUST IN GOD

~~~~~

*Can I really trust God? If I do, what if he
doesn't come through for me?*

Coaching is in my blood. If I were not a pastor, I guarantee you I would be on the sidelines of a football field calling plays. Before sensing a call to ministry, that's exactly what I thought I'd be doing. I wanted to play college football and coach high school football. I had dreams of leading a team out on the field for some *Friday Night Lights* action.

Clear eyes.

Full heart.

Can't lose.[1]

Sorry, I get carried away when I think about coaching. My dad coached many of my childhood teams, and I knew that when our daughters got to the age where they were involved in sports, I'd be their coach. I was so into this that all our girls' names are athletic names.

Some people name their children after relatives they love or people they admire or because of what the names actually mean. I named our children based off what their names would sound like over a PA system when they were scoring goals or accepting all-state honors in high school. I'm serious. Just listen to these names and convince me that you can't imagine the crowds cheering after hearing them:

"Riley Steeeeeeeephens!"

"Kelsey Steeeeeeeephens!"

"Cameron Steeeeeeeephens!"

"Landry Steeeeeeeephens!"

I get goose bumps just imagining it! But for them to be that successful, they needed their dad coaching them on the fundamentals. At least that was my thinking. I was willing to coach them in any sport they wanted to play except soccer. I never played soccer. I don't like soccer. I don't watch soccer. I don't know the rules for soccer. Count me out on any sport that takes hours to play and usually ends in a score of 1-0. Heck, soccer wasn't even considered a sport when I was growing up back in Louisiana.

Riley wanted to play T-ball, so I gladly signed up to coach her team. We were one of the only co-ed T-ball teams in the league. We would show up, and I could overhear the first-grade boys from the other team making fun of having to play a team with a bunch of girls. We didn't win many games that year, but we did surprise some people and squeak out a few wins.

Kelsey wanted to play basketball. Fine by me! We signed her up, and I coached her team for a little while. I learned from my mistakes with Riley's team and recruited hard for Kelsey's first- and second-grade basketball team. I had coaches wanting to check birth certificates because of two of the girls we signed up to play. I'm pretty sure that Lady Lightning won the championship that year!

Then the twins came along. And wouldn't you know it, they wanted to play soccer. I didn't know whether to be disappointed, disgusted, or both. This was not the type of *fútbol* I had in mind when I first dreamed of coaching.

I had sworn that I would not coach stupid soccer. But then I realized that Cameron and Landry would be practicing or playing in games every Saturday morning. Someone was going to get to be with them. Someone was going to get to teach them. Someone was going to get to watch them up close as they learned something new and had fun doing it. Someone was going to be able to run out on the field when they fell and skinned a knee and tell them it would be okay.

I *knew* I had to be that someone. I wasn't going to miss that opportunity to be close to my girls and get the closest view of their cute little faces. I wanted to be the first one they ran to when they scored a goal. I wanted to be the one who lifted them up after we won the league championship. I wanted to be the one they looked to if they got nervous or intimidated. I loved these girls and wanted them to see me on their turf, playing with and caring for them.

So, even though it was a dumb sport, if the twins wanted to play dumb soccer, I would be the dumb coach.

It couldn't be that hard anyway, right? Kick the tiny ball into the tiny goal. I could show them how to kick a ball. What really mattered to me was our team name. This is where the motivation starts for five- and six-year-olds! Next to the snacks at the end of the game, it's probably the main thing they get excited about. My wife came through big-time on this one. She came up with the name the Kickin' Chickens.

I showed up for the first practice not knowing one soccer drill to do with the team. I still hardly understood any of the rules of the game. But I had a blast! I started looking forward to each Saturday watching our little team get after it.

I kept my composure for the most part when we lost.

I didn't lose my cool—too badly—when other teams didn't properly substitute.

I may or may not have had to assure the girls that I wasn't yelling at them—that I was just passionate and excited about the game.

And I continually had to remind myself that it was five- and six-year-old soccer, not tryouts for FC Barcelona.

Who knew that a dumb game could be so much fun! My favorite part of every practice and game ended the same way: we would stack our hands on top of one another, and I told the girls that I wanted the neighbors to hear us as we screamed on the count of three, "Kickin' Chickens, bok bok!"

There is no doubt that some people watching me coach thought I was crazy. You might even say over the top. Maybe I was. But really I was over the top for Landry and Cameron. I wanted them to have a good time. Coaching was just a way for me to be close to them, watch them, invest in them, and show my love for them.

TRUST AND ENTRUST

I have repeatedly written two words in the margins of my Bible: *trust* and *entrust*. They make up a recurring theme in Scripture. We are called over and over to trust God and entrust our lives to him.

I liken the difference between these two words to an illustration I once heard about Charles Blondin, who walked a wheelbarrow on a tightrope across Niagara Falls. A crowd gathered to watch him achieve this feat, and when it was over, Blondin asked them if they believed that he could walk the wheelbarrow back to the other side. When the cheering crowd answered yes, Blondin then asked, "Who will get in the wheelbarrow?"[2]

We are to trust God by relying on and believing in him. We are to entrust our lives to him by surrendering totally and completely to his will and his ways. Let me give you a few examples from Scripture.

The Israelites were escaping from being enslaved by the Egyptians. Pharaoh changed his mind and led his army after them. The Hebrew people were trapped. On one side was the Red Sea; on the other was Pharaoh's army. What was God's message for the people? Trust and entrust.

Do not be afraid. Stand firm and you will see the deliverance the LORD will bring you today. The Egyptians you see today you will never see again. The LORD will fight for you; you need only to be still. (Exodus 14:13–14)

They had demonstrated trust in following Moses out of Egypt, and now they needed to entrust their lives to God and watch him deliver them. They didn't need to come up with a plan. They didn't need to try to get out of their predicament themselves. God was calling them to trust him and entrust their lives to him.

What about a situation like this? Your boss gives someone in your office the promotion you were supposed to get. You were the one working hard, always going the extra mile, yet you didn't get it. How should you respond? Trust and entrust.

No one from the east or the west
    or from the desert can exalt themselves.
It is God who judges:
    He brings one down, he exalts another. (Psalm 75:6–7)

You've been walking with God in faithfulness. You have honored him in your work ethic. You have trusted him with your entire career. What do you do now that you didn't get the promotion? You trust that his will is being done, and you keep entrusting your life and career to him. It's ultimately not your boss who didn't exalt you in this way at this time; it was God. And he can be trusted.

What about when you suffer? How should you posture your heart when you're in the heat of persecution or the middle of a trial? Trust and entrust. Just like Jesus.

To this you were called, because Christ suffered for you, leaving you an example, that you should follow in his steps.

"He committed no sin,
   and no deceit was found in his mouth."

When they hurled their insults at him, he did not retaliate;
when he suffered, he made no threats. Instead, he entrusted
himself to him who judges justly. (1 Peter 2:21–23)

Jesus trusted his Father and entrusted his life to him, even if it
meant suffering. When you think about it, there is no greater
demonstration of trust than when we entrust our lives completely to God and his will being done, even if it means suffering.

We may not have all the answers. We may not understand
what God is doing or why. But, good news, he never asks us to.
He asks us to do two things: trust him and entrust our lives to
him.

I find two images in the Bible so incredibly meaningful. Whenever I read them in Scripture, they seem to build the trust muscle
that makes my faith in God stronger.

GOD AS FATHER

The first image is of a *father.*

It may be difficult for you to embrace the image of God as a
father. It could be that your dad was abusive or neglectful. He
may not have come through on his promises or even been involved in your life at all. If this is your story, I understand why the
father image can be hard to embrace.

Fortunately, God is the *perfect* father. He's not like your dad.
He never makes mistakes. He always leads us in the right direction. He knows when we need discipline and what discipline
would be most effective. As we have seen, he is a father whose
eyes are always on us, whose ears are always open to us, and
who always speaks words of love, encouragement, and affirma-

tion. God is not like the father of your childhood; he is a perfect father.

He's a "good, good father." Sorry, I was having a Chris Tomlin moment.[3] (If you thought that was bad, you should see when I have a DC Talk moment. And if you don't know who they are, that's a spiritual problem. You may need to repent.)

Jesus introduced this concept of God as father in the Sermon on the Mount. Seventeen times in this sermon, he repeats the message that God is our father. I think this was his way of convincing people that God could be trusted. He was changing the way they thought about him.

God's not aloof like the people might have imagined.

He's not judgmental like the religious leadership they were familiar with.

He's not a taskmaster like the Roman authorities.

Jesus taught them that God is a father, which means *he can be trusted*. Trusted to provide and meet your most basic physical needs. Trusted to provide and meet your deepest spiritual needs. I love Eugene Peterson's paraphrase of what Jesus said in this sermon:

> There is far more to your life than the food you put in your stomach, more to your outer appearance than the clothes you hang on your body. Look at the birds, free and unfettered, not tied down to a job description, careless in the care of God. And you count far more to him than birds. (Matthew 6:25–26, MSG)

Beautiful! We can be "careless in the care of God." God can be trusted for food. He can be trusted for clothing. If he takes care of the birds, he will take care of us.

Jesus spoke these words to people who had serious concerns. Most were poor and impoverished. One of the decisions I make on a daily basis is where I'm going to eat. I don't have to wonder *if* I'm going to eat. Those listening to Jesus that day really didn't know where their next meal would come from. The thought of not being able to eat or provide for their families worried them.

Jesus wanted them to know that they didn't need to waste time worrying, because God is a father and can be trusted.

Think about all the needless worrying we do. The other day I went to WebMD to check out some side effects for medicine I was taking. Bad idea! I began feeling new side effects I hadn't experienced before reading the list in the first place!

Listen to what WebMD states about worry:

> Chronic worrying can affect your daily life so much that it may interfere with your appetite, lifestyle habits, relationships, sleep, and job performance. Many people who worry excessively are so anxiety-ridden that they seek relief in harmful lifestyle habits such as overeating, cigarette smoking, or using alcohol and drugs. . . . Anxiety disorders are commonplace in the U.S., affecting nearly 40 million adults.[4]

The National Center for Health Statistics reported that more than 13 percent of American adults are taking some form of an antidepressant.[5] According to the National Institute of Mental Health, depression affects some seventeen million American adults a year.[6] A *Time* magazine article stated that depression costs the US up to $210 billion annually in health-care needs.[7]

Those numbers reveal that worry was not just an issue for people in the time of Jesus; it's an issue in our time as well.

In this same sermon, Jesus said that worrying doesn't help us at all. It doesn't add an hour to our lives or an inch to our height (Matthew 6:27).

So, what's the answer? I don't want to sound simplistic, but I really believe the answer now is the same as it was then. It's trust and entrust, and we can do this because we have God as our father.

I remember when I was teaching Landry how to swim. I couldn't wait until she was old enough and could swim well enough for me to launch her in the air as high as I could and listen to her scream. I had done this with her older sisters, and I was going to do it with her, too. But she had to learn to swim first. I can remember inviting her into the pool with me, holding my arms stretched toward her. All she had to do was jump in. Dad was going to catch her.

This would go on for what seemed like hours. She wanted me to be closer to her. She wanted me to hold her. All I wanted from her was for her to jump in, trusting that I would catch her. She kept telling me how afraid she was. She would walk up and down on the side of the pool and throw a bit of a tantrum. A stranger watching would have thought I was trying to kidnap her, not teach her to swim!

Her hesitancy to trust me caused me to question my past actions. Had I done something to make her doubt my reliability as her dad? Mentally, I started going through a checklist:

She has never missed a meal—ever. *Check.*

She has always had clothes to wear. *Check.*

There was that one time I forgot to pick her up from school, but that was just a miscommunication between her mom and me. Not taking the blame for that one!

She has always had a bed to sleep in and a roof over her head. *Check.*

She has never witnessed me tossing one of her sisters in the air and then just walking away. *Check.*

I didn't know why she wouldn't trust me. Somehow, in her mind, her fear was bigger than I was.

That's our problem with trusting God: life gets complex, and a lot of times what we are up against seems bigger than him.

The point Jesus was driving home in the Sermon on the Mount is the same point he wants to drive home with us. God made the world out of nothing. He clothes the fields of the grass. He feeds the birds of the air. He created and sustains you. No problem we face is bigger than our heavenly Father. He can be trusted.

Paul wrote to the church in Philippi, "My God will meet all your needs according to the riches of his glory in Christ Jesus" (Philippians 4:19).

GOD AS SHEPHERD

The second image of God that is so attractive to me is that of a *shepherd*. I admit, I feel a little weird using the words *attractive* and *shepherd* in the same sentence. Part of it is that I don't think I've ever even seen a shepherd in real life! But I love the picture we get of a shepherd in the Bible, for instance in Psalm 23.

Psalm 23 is read at funerals and quoted on battlefields. I've seen it drawn on the walls of nurseries and definitely have heard it preached on. The overarching themes of this beloved psalm are that a shepherd has the responsibility to guide his sheep and that sheep have the responsibility to follow the shepherd. Because God is the "Chief Shepherd" (1 Peter 5:4) of our souls, he will take care of us and we can trust him and entrust our lives to him.

> The LORD is my shepherd, I lack nothing.
>   He makes me lie down in green pastures,
> he leads me beside quiet waters,
>   he refreshes my soul.
> He guides me along the right paths
>   for his name's sake.
> Even though I walk
>   through the darkest valley,

I will fear no evil,
>   for you are with me;
your rod and your staff,
>   they comfort me.

You prepare a table before me
>   in the presence of my enemies.
You anoint my head with oil;
>   my cup overflows.
Surely your goodness and love will follow me
>   all the days of my life,
and I will dwell in the house of the LORD
>   forever." (Psalm 23)

When I read this, I think, *Wow, I didn't realize it, but my soul needs a shepherd!* The psalm helps us understand what God, our shepherd, does for us as he guides us in life. It's amazing when you think about it.

First, God acts as our *personal shepherd*.

Did you notice that David, the author of the psalm, used the personal pronoun *my* to describe his relationship with God? I love that! Jesus referred to himself as our "good shepherd" (John 10:11–15) and explained that he is a personal shepherd as opposed to some uncaring guy who is simply hired to watch after the sheep.

A personal shepherd *personally* cares for his sheep. Unlike someone who is hired to look after the sheep, the shepherd is willing to lay his life down for them. Being a personal shepherd is not just a job; it's his life. The personal shepherd is known by his tender care for the sheep.

I like to think of myself as a relatively tough guy. (Well, I may not be that tough, but I don't take bubble baths!) Yet I will admit that the idea of having someone who loves me and wants to tenderly care for me sounds pretty great. How about for you?

And it's not just that he's a personal shepherd.

Second, he guides the sheep to find *rest and refreshment*.

The shepherd in Psalm 23 leads the sheep to "green pastures" and "quiet waters," which represent security and renewal. The word *refresh* the psalmist uses actually means to "turn back."[8] As sheep, we tend to go our own way, which is often the wrong and dangerous way. Well, I'll speak for me: I tend to go my own way and usually discover it's the wrong way. I don't know you, but if you're like everyone I know, you do the same. That's why we need God to be our shepherd who turns us back to himself and leads us along right paths.

Third, he guides the sheep to find *right paths*.

Even when we go through dark valleys and times of loneliness, we don't have to fear or worry. Why? Because God is our shepherd and is with us and guiding us, even in the darkest times.

Fourth, he guides the sheep to find *refuge*.

The shepherd has a rod and staff. The idea is that God will not let danger in. While our enemy tries to take from us, God our shepherd is taking care of us. Even when we walk through dark valleys, our safety, security, and well-being are his priority.

Max Lucado wrote about the idea of God being a shepherd:

> What a surprising way to describe God! We're accustomed to a God who remains in one place. A God who sits enthroned in the heavens and rules and ordains. David, however, envisions a mobile and active God. Dare we do the same? Dare we envision a God who follows us? Who pursues us? Who chases us? Who tracks us down and wins us over? Who follows us with "goodness and mercy" all the days of our lives?[9]

So, the shepherd's responsibility is to guide the sheep. But we're the sheep; what's our responsibility?

WE AS SHEEP

The sheep follow the shepherd. Uh-oh. This is where we have an issue. Sheep have a following problem. I don't know if it's universally true, but I've found that most often the root of a following problem is a trusting problem. Just like Landry not wanting to jump into my arms, the issue at the end of the day is a lack of trust. We don't trust, so we don't really follow. We are straying sheep (1 Peter 2:25). Isaiah the prophet said it like this: "We all, like sheep, have gone astray, each of us has turned to our own way" (Isaiah 53:6).

I told you I have never seen a shepherd, and I will admit I have seen very few sheep. But shepherds and sheep are mentioned so many times in the Bible that you kind of have to study them to get your pastor's license. As I've learned about sheep, I've discovered how apt the comparison to people is. Why? Well . . .

Sheep Are Easily Distracted

Sheep are known for not paying attention. Me too! How about you? (I have to admit, in the middle of typing this paragraph, I checked my email and Twitter. Ugh.)

Distraction is one of the strategies Satan uses against us. If he can distract us from really thinking about God as our shepherd, he can erode our trust in God and create a following problem.

So he throws entertainment at us.

He throws busyness at us.

He'll make us think that God is holding out on us.

He will do anything he can to distract us from thinking of God as our shepherd. He will do everything in his power to call us away, create some distance, or cause us to forget that God is our personal shepherd who loves and guides us.

We sheep are so easily distracted. I wonder what Satan's been doing to divert your attention away from God and his care for you. Do you know?

It'd be enough if we were just easily distracted, but there's more.

Sheep Are Easily Deceived

Jesus warned his followers of false teachers who would come along and try to deceive us. He said, "Watch out for false prophets. They come to you in sheep's clothing, but inwardly they are ferocious wolves" (Matthew 7:15).

These false teachers will tempt us to put our trust in someone other than God. They will teach half truths and pretend they really care. Think of all the world religions and cults that people embrace. Go back to their beginnings, and the premises always start with not trusting the always God. Satan, who is behind all these false religions, wants to deceive people, making them think that God can't be trusted and shouldn't be followed.

Unfortunately, it's not just false teachers and false religions. We can be deceived by well-meaning family or friends who think that they are giving us good advice but are actually steering us away from God's will. Life following Jesus is often countercultural and counterintuitive, so commonsense advice can often run counter to the truth.

To prevent being deceived, we need to develop the skill of knowing and hearing the true Shepherd's voice. Jesus said it like this: "His sheep follow him because they know his voice. But they will never follow a stranger; in fact, they will run away from him because they do not recognize a stranger's voice" (John 10:4–5).

Sheep are easily distracted.

Sheep are easily deceived.

And . . .

Sheep Are Easily Distressed

We sheep have short memories. We forget how God our shepherd has provided for us in the past. We forget how he has guided us through some pretty rough waters and dark valleys. When we get distressed, instead of recalling the faithfulness of our shepherd, we focus on the fears and worries of life. Distress overtakes trust. You've been there, right? I don't just mean at some point in your life. I mean, you've been there *this week,* right? Remember, we decided we're going to be completely honest with each other. We all forget, we get distressed, and distress overwhelms trust.

So, how can we learn to turn this around?

COFFEE-CUP CHRISTIANITY

When you go to write a book like this, you pitch the publishers a few ideas you are working on. A friend gave me the idea to write a book about well-known Bible verses—scriptures we know by heart and have seen on coffee cups and picture frames or heard quoted by celebrities at press conferences and award ceremonies.

We have all seen John 3:16 written in bold on a banner at an NFL game. We have all heard 1 Corinthians 13 quoted by the presiding minister at a wedding. Many of us have repeated the words of Jeremiah 29:11 to comfort friends whose dreams just died or who are wondering about their future.

We know these verses and are quick to quote them to give inspiration and encouragement, but sometimes we don't know their context. Instead of digging into the Bible to really understand them, we're content if their context is simply a mug. It's coffee-cup Christianity.

One of these verses you've seen and probably quoted is "Trust in the LORD with all your heart, and do not lean on your own understanding. In all your ways acknowledge him, and he will make straight your paths" (Proverbs 3:5–6, ESV).

What is God asking us to do? Trust and entrust. This is our responsibility. But let's make sure we really understand what this verse is saying.

I went to the Apple Store a couple of years ago to get my then thirteen-year-old her first phone. You know how it is with technology today. Whenever you make a purchase, you have to agree to the terms and conditions. Can I make a confession? They put those conditions in front of me and I never read them! Like ever. The print is way too small. There is too much to read. Typically, I'm in a hurry. I always sign it, but for all I know, I could be agreeing to sell my house or my firstborn! I asked the woman serving us that day if she's ever had anyone actually read through the terms and conditions. Her response? "Never." I didn't feel so bad, and some of you can stop judging me, because you know you never read the terms and conditions either!

In this proverb, we need to read the terms and conditions of the promise God makes to us. His promise is to make our paths straight. It's a picture of a construction crew cutting a road where there is currently no road. Incredible!

We can be up against the wall.

Our situation can look like it's a dead end.

The relationship we're in can seem over.

But God promises that he will make a way. He will cut a road where there is no road. We can trust him to do this.

But there are terms and conditions we have to agree to. What are they?

Trust.

Lean.

Know.

We are to *trust* in the LORD with all our hearts. LORD is written in all caps, reminding us whom we are putting our trust in. LORD is how our English Bible translates "Yahweh," the name that Israel's covenant God goes by. Solomon is the wisest man to ever live, and he was really wise in writing this verse. We're not just putting our trust in anyone; we are putting our trust in the LORD.

When we begin to understand who the LORD is and what he has done in the past, trusting in him is really not that hard at all.

The LORD has always delivered.

The LORD has always kept his word.

The LORD has always come through.

He is the always God. It's easy to trust the LORD when you are walking in a relationship with him.

Another term and condition we need to agree to if God is to come through on his promise is to *lean*. The first term is stated in the positive—"Trust in the LORD." The second term is stated in the negative—"Do not lean on your own understanding."

The word *lean* means to "rest upon" or "place confidence in."[10] In Bible times, kings or military leaders were said to lean on the arm of a trusted associate or friend (2 Kings 5:18; 7:2, 17). They counted on their friends. They needed their counsel. They relied on them. We are not to lean on our own understanding; instead, we are to trust God with all our hearts.

Trust and entrust. This verse amplifies the fact that sometimes we don't know what is best for our lives. I don't know about you, but I can't trust myself to say no to a second piece of pie! I prove all the time that I am not the best decision maker for my life. I'm not smart enough to know what's best for me. Half the time, I need my oldest to show me how to work my smart TV. So, we should not lean on our own understanding.

That is hard to do, isn't it?

When a challenging situation arises or we face a decision, our inclination is to make a list of positives and negatives. We think about what will benefit us the most. We call our friends and get their input. We do all that *before* taking it to the Lord.

This is leaning on our own understanding, and it can cause us trouble if we are trusting our understanding more than we're trusting God. Solomon warns of this in other proverbs:

> There is a way that seems right to a man,
>   but its end is the way to death. (14:12, ESV)

> Whoever trusts in his own mind is a fool. (28:26, ESV)

Sometimes when we come to a fork in the road concerning a decision, everything seems to be telling us to go a certain direction.

Our heads.

Our hearts.

Our friends.

All pointing in one direction. It feels right. It seems logical. It makes sense. But we need to exercise caution. Solomon says that the wrong decision can lead to death. Be careful leaning on your own understanding.

> "My thoughts are not your thoughts,
>   neither are your ways my ways,"
>   declares the LORD.
> "As the heavens are higher than the earth,
>   so are my ways higher than your ways
>   and my thoughts than your thoughts." (Isaiah 55:8–9)

Sometimes God will lead you to do the opposite of what your heart, your head, and your friends counsel. If you want him to cut a path, you can't lean on your own understanding. You have to trust and lean on him.

The final term and condition we have to sign off on for this promise to go into effect is to *know*.

Solomon calls us to make sure we "acknowledge him" (Proverbs 3:6, ESV) in all our ways. *Acknowledge* is translated from the Hebrew word *yada*. It refers to a personal knowledge and is used in other places in Scripture to describe God's knowledge of us.[11]

How does God acknowledge, or know, us? Inside and out. The Bible tells us in Psalm 44:21 that he *yada* ("knows") the secrets of our hearts. The Bible also tells us in Psalm 139:4 that before a word is on our tongues, he *yada* ("knows") it.

God knows us better than we know ourselves, and he is calling for what A. W. Tozer termed a "positive reciprocation."[12] Just as God knows us, we are called to know him. We are told in Psalm 9:10 that those who *yada* ("know") God's name will put their trust in him.

When we commit to trusting, leaning on, and knowing him, he *will* make our paths straight. He has promised that if he has to, he will cut a road where there is no road.

WHAT DO I DO?

Since I was seventeen years old, my goal was to be a pastor. I was asked to lead a Bible study in my senior year of high school, and as I studied to teach the lesson that week, God turned my heart toward ministry. It's all I've known career-wise. I love the local church and wanted to lead a local church.

After serving on staff at my former church for eight years as the young-singles-and-college pastor, a church from another state called to ask if I would consider coming to be its lead pastor.

I loved the church I was serving and wasn't looking to leave. However, this church called, and something in my heart leaped. I liked the area where the church was located. The church was going to allow me to build a team, adding certain needed staff members. There was money in the church's bank account and no debt. It seemed God might be in this.

The search committee wanted to meet with me and my wife.

We decided it was worth looking into, so we met on several occasions. We really enjoyed their company. I took a tour of the church one evening and could imagine myself leading that congregation.

Everything about it felt right except for one small hesitation: it just didn't seem like God was releasing me from the church I was already serving at. I didn't understand why. It seemed as though the stars were all aligning. I wanted to pastor a church, and a church wanted me to be its pastor. My wife was ready and willing to go. I felt I had reached my lid at my current church and was looking for a new assignment. The only position that interested me at my current church was the teaching-pastor role, but we had a seasoned leader in that position.

I remember praying about it. Unfortunately, I have had times when I just went with what felt right or made decisions based on my selfish desires. But this time I knew I had to be in the will of God. I think in this case God probably would have been fine with either decision, but I wanted too much to do what he wanted.

Proverbs 3:5–6 guided me through this time. I realized that whatever decision I made would require trust.

I had never been a lead pastor. Stepping out in this way was a big decision and would require a lot of trust.

Staying in my role and continuing what I had been doing the previous eight years with no promise or path to something else would require some trust as well.

I didn't know what to do. I was jogging one evening, praying and thinking about the choice I had to make. That's when God spoke to my heart. It became one of those moments. I could take you to the neighborhood I was running in and the house I was running by when I sensed that God was speaking in my spirit these words: *What's it going to take more faith to do?*

Either choice I made would take a step of faith and trust in God, but I realized it would take more trust in God to stay in the seat I was in.

A part of me felt like I was putting my dream on hold. I didn't understand why I never felt a peace about leaving. I can say with confidence that I was living out Proverbs 3:5–6.

I was trusting God.

I wasn't leaning on my own understanding.

I had vowed to know him and keep growing in my relationship with him.

Bottom line: I agreed to all the terms and conditions in these verses. And you know what? God kept his promise.

A few weeks later, the teaching pastor at my church relocated. The position opened, and the senior pastor asked me to take it. Wow! For ten years, I got to lead, preach, and have influence in ways I never would have if I had left.

God cut a path, and I love the road he has me on.

That story has a nice bow on it. It's a sweet story to tell when you're sharing coffee in mugs with Bible verses on them. It's a sweet story to tell now. But in the middle, it wasn't sweet; it was sweaty! I felt scared and stuck, and I was struggling to sense God's shepherding.

I say that because you may still be in the middle of your story. In the middle, it's hard to believe there will be a happy ending. In fact, in the middle, you can think you're at the ending and it can feel pretty crappy, not happy. I get it. I was there. It was hard, but I chose to trust and entrust, believing that God would be faithful.

You can do the same.

Trust and entrust. God is faithful.

CHAPTER 12

HOPE IN GOD

~~~~~~

I want to put my hope in God,
but what if he disappoints me?

I am adopted.

Please don't tell my parents.

Dick and Marvel De Witt adopted me. Not officially, but I do have a certificate they printed and gave me naming me as such. While it may not hold legal status, I'm proud to be their adopted son. I've known Dick and Marvel for close to ten years. They moved to Plano, Texas, in 2006 and joined our church shortly thereafter. To know them is to love them. And speaking of love, they have quite the love story.

They both grew up and went to high school in Clarence, New York. They didn't date in high school. They knew each other but didn't run in the same circles. Dick was a few years older than Marvel, and they were pretty different. Dick played golf and was a bit quieter and more reserved. Marvel was a cheerleader, a popular girl, and a motivated student.

They began dating a few years later after they ran into each other on Marvel's first day of college. Marvel purposely chose a college that none of her high school friends were attending. Being the first in her family to attend a university, she made up her mind to not allow any distractions to take her away from her studies. She was determined to earn good grades, get her degree, and make her family proud.

On her first day at the State University of New York at Oswego, Marvel registered for her classes and then headed back to her dorm with her roommate. That's when they crossed paths with Dick. They had not seen each other since high school, and Dick promptly asked, "Marvel Young, what are you doing here?" Marvel responded in her quick-witted way, "Richard De Witt, what are *you* doing here?" They started dating soon after. So much for Marvel's plan to not allow any distractions!

They dated throughout college, were married in 1968, and then moved to New Jersey. Dick got a job in New York City, and Marvel taught elementary school. They welcomed their first child, Kurt, into the world in 1970. He was a happy, outgoing, adventurous child. They were a picture-perfect little family.

Two years later, Dick took a job in Jacksonville, Florida. They moved south and at the same time added a daughter to their family. Amy was born in 1974.

God did a miracle with Amy's birth. Actually, he did two miracles. During the pregnancy, the doctors told Dick and Marvel that there was only a one-in-five chance the baby would survive. So it was a miracle she was born and was healthy. God did the second miracle through the pediatrician, a believer who faithfully prayed for and shared his faith with Dick and Marvel. Dick and Marvel were always churchgoers but didn't know what it meant to have a personal relationship with Jesus. Through the witness of this doctor and going through the trial of a tough pregnancy, Dick and Marvel put their trust in Jesus.

They eventually moved to Buffalo, New York, so Dick could take over the family food business. They were a sailing family. Dick loved being on the water. Living near Lake Ontario, they had a couple of sailboats. Dick named the second one *Marvelus*.

They were a happy family, living the American dream. They were involved in church. They were leaders in their community. Life could not have been any better.

THE PHONE CALL

On August 14, 1997, Dick and Marvel received the phone call every parent dreads.

That weekend, Kurt was the best man in a friend's wedding. This was the fourth time he would serve as best man. That was Kurt: a best friend to many. He was outgoing like his mom. He was a leader like his dad. Kurt had called his dad earlier in the week to see if he wanted to take the Coast Guard captain's license qualifying course together. Dick quickly agreed.

Kurt was out with a friend of his when a drunk-driving accident caused the car he was in to crash in a deep ditch. The impact killed Kurt. He was twenty-six years old with his entire life ahead of him. The next few days were a whirlwind for Dick, Marvel, and Amy. More than four thousand people came to the visitation and funeral.

Dick and Marvel say that it was only their faith in Christ and their faith community that got them through this torturous time in their lives.

Dick and Marvel began speaking at schools through Impact Panels and Prom Promise events, warning kids of the dangers of driving while intoxicated. Embracing a mission in the midst of the unexplainable helped their grieving process.

Amy was busy graduating from college. She chose to follow in the footsteps of her mom and teach elementary school. She met JP, fell in love, and married him in 2001. Amy and JP ultimately gave Dick and Marvel three beautiful grandchildren.

In 2006, Dick and Marvel made their final move, going to Texas to follow Dick's call into full-time ministry. He served as the executive president and COO of Marketplace Ministries, placing chaplains in businesses all across North America. He joined our church, serving as a leader in various capacities, including chairman of the deacons. Marvel sings in our choir each week.

In 2015, Amy began experiencing some pain and went to the doctor. After running some tests, doctors diagnosed her with a rare form of sarcoma and gave her only nine months to live. Amy immediately began treatment, and everyone started praying for her healing.

I met Amy on a number of occasions when she was in town visiting her mom and dad. She loved attending our church's Christmas program. She was always so full of life. I thought of Amy as my adopted sister, so I felt led to focus my prayers on her. I also wrote her name beside certain passages in my Bible. I was confident that God would heal her. Knowing what Dick and Marvel had already been through with Kurt, I thought there was no way God would take Amy, too.

NOT AGAIN

I will never forget receiving the text from Dick on Friday night, May 8, 2020, around ten fifteen at night. It simply read, "Amy is home."

Four and a half years after her diagnosis, Amy slipped into the presence of Jesus. She left behind Dick and Marvel; her husband, JP; and their children, Andrew, Grace, and Will.

After being diagnosed with cancer, Amy asked me to preach her funeral. I told her I would, but in my heart I really didn't think the day would come. She had so many people praying for her healing, her entire life to live, and three children to raise.

I struggled as I wrote the message for her funeral. To be clear, I wrestled not with what I would say about Amy or God but with what the Bible tells those who grieve. Paul instructs the church in Thessalonica, "Brothers and sisters, we do not want you to be uninformed about those who sleep in death, so that you do not grieve like the rest of mankind, who have no hope" (1 Thessalonians 4:13).

"No hope." I was supposed to tell those gathered at the funeral that we grieve but with hope. The Bible says that we still have hope. I knew I would faithfully tell them what the Bible says, but honestly I didn't know if I believed it in the moment. I also wondered if Dick and Marvel still believed it.

HOPE HAS A ROPE

Hope has been called oxygen for the soul. I've heard it said that humans can live thirty days without food, three days without water, and three minutes without air, but we cannot live three seconds without hope.[1]

Billy Graham traveled to more than 185 countries and territories all over the world, preaching to at least 215 million people.[2] In his book *Hope for the Troubled Heart,* he wrote,

> In my travels over the decades, I have found that people are the same the world over. However, in recent years I find that there is an increasing problem that I would sum up in the word "hopeless." . . .
>
> Perhaps the greatest psychological, spiritual, and medical need that all people have is the need for hope.[3]

He wrote that in 1991, but it reads like it could have been written yesterday. So many people feel hopeless.

When a relationship fails or a spouse is unfaithful, you can feel hopeless.

When the company downsizes and your job falls through, you can feel hopeless.

When your teenager starts going down a wrong path, you can feel hopeless.

When your health deteriorates and your body starts to fail, you can feel hopeless.

When a global pandemic hits and uncertainties abound, you can feel hopeless.

Where do we turn when we have these feelings of hopelessness?

In the Old Testament, we read about Job, a man who lost everything. He lost his children, his fortune, and his health. He was feeling hopeless and turned to his wife and friends for comfort. You know what he was feeling after listening to them? Even more hopeless!

Job turned to people; others turn to substances in a desperate grab for hope. But the drugs, alcohol, or pornography never delivers on what it promises, and people just end up feeling more hopeless than before.

Some people turn to the church to get rid of the nagging sense of hopelessness. They come looking for a peace that they've heard their mom and dad or friends talk about. It may be a last-resort search for a "higher power" to "do his thing" and provide some much-needed hope. It's sad, but I've heard stories of people who, instead of being filled with hope, leave depressed and discouraged because the church gave them just a list of rules to follow or activities to perform.

When he was feeling hopeless, the psalmist turned inward and asked himself, "Why, my soul, are you downcast? Why so disturbed within me? Put your hope in God" (Psalm 42:5).

When we feel hopeless, we should turn to God. Our hope in him is like an anchor that keeps a boat from drifting.

I thought about hope being like an anchor last year when I was asked to teach a chapel service for kindergartners and first graders. My former church has an affiliated school, and from time to time I was asked to speak at the Lower School's chapel. Each week, hundreds of students came together to sing songs and hear a devotional thought from the Bible. The school assigned me the topic of hope.

People often ask me if I ever get nervous before speaking. The truth is that I do sometimes—except when I speak to children. I am nervous *every time* I speak to children. Don't ask me why, but I would rather preach to a coliseum full of people than a small room full of first graders.

After teaching the chapel service for a number of years, I had developed a system for speaking to the kids. First, you need to have an object lesson. No orator is skilled enough to keep the attention of kindergartners and first graders for long without an object lesson. Second, you must have a short statement that the students can easily repeat. Bonus points if it rhymes. Third, and perhaps most important, you cannot under any circumstance ask an open-ended question. That's a recipe for disaster, every time.

I racked my brain that week, getting ready to teach the elementary school kids about hope. Finally, I had an illustration. I would tie one side of a rope around my waist and ask a first grader to tie the other side around his waist. I also came up with a short rhyming statement that the kids could repeat: "Hope has a rope." And there was no way I would ask an open-ended question. I set myself up for guaranteed success!

The lesson was simple. I stood onstage. I told the kids that I represented God. A first grader came up onstage. I explained that he represented people. The rope demonstrated that when we are tied to God, in a relationship with him, there is always hope. I told the kid tied to me to run around and try his best to cause me to move. I outweighed the first grader by more than a hundred pounds! There was nothing he could do to make me budge. The kids all got a kick out of watching their classmate strain to try to pull away from me. He couldn't because I had him anchored to me. Our always God is *always* our anchor.

The kids seemed to get it, but in real life we can't see an actual rope holding us to God. Sometimes our problems seem so intrusive and enlarged that it's hard for us to see God at all and we think there is no way God is anchoring us on the other side.

But it's true: hope always has a rope. Why don't you say that out loud? C'mon, if the kindergartners can, you can too. Say it loud and proud:

Hope has a rope.

REMINDERS

I have a short list of the greatest inventions of all time. First, the air conditioner. I truly can't comprehend how my parents grew up without it. Second, TiVo. I cannot calculate the joy it brings me to fast-forward through commercials. The third-greatest invention? The reminders we can set on our phones.

This invention ended writing birthdays and anniversaries down in a daily planner. If you are a millennial or Gen Zer, a daily planner was a printed calendar people carried around in a nice leather-bound notebook. Sounds crazy, right?

I love the reminder setting. You put the date, time, and event in your calendar, and your phone will remind you one week, one day, one hour, or fifteen minutes before it happens. I don't even have to remember my anniversary anymore. Reminders are the best!

In the Old Testament, God gave the people of Israel a reminder at a time when they desperately needed it.

God allowed Nebuchadnezzar, the evil king of Babylon, to capture the Jewish people as a consequence for their sin. God then spoke to the prophet Jeremiah, letting him know that Israel would be in captivity for the next seventy years. To the Jewish people, this felt like a life sentence. For some of them, it *was* a life sentence.

Can you imagine the despair they must have felt? They would not see their homeland for seventy years! Some would die not in the beloved city of Jerusalem but instead in the pagan land of Babylon. They would no longer be able to freely worship God. They had to live in a foreign land among people who worshipped false gods. They must have felt utterly hopeless.

Yet in the midst of this, God showed up with a word for the people. God told them through Jeremiah, "I know the plans I have for you, . . . plans to prosper you and not to harm you, plans to give you hope and a future" (29:11).

That reminder God gave to the people of Israel is one that I believe he wants to give *you.*

I'll paraphrase what he was telling them but in first person so you can internalize it when you read it:

God loves me and is for me.

If we were sitting together at a Starbucks, I'd ask you to say that out loud, even though it would be cheesy. I'd want you to hear the words. So, could I ask you to read those words out loud? Here they are again:

God loves me and is for me.

At Starbucks, even though I'd hope that I wasn't being annoying, I'd ask you to say them out loud one more time, just to really convince yourself. Any chance I could get you to do that? One more time:

God loves me and is for me.

If that's true, it changes everything. And it is true. And it's amazing! Remember, God gave that message through Jeremiah when his people were at their worst. God loved his people even in their sin and rebellion. Yes, they experienced his judgment. God disciplines those he loves (Hebrews 12:5–11), but he never stops loving those who are in relationship with him. And he is always for those in relationship with him.

That's true for you. God loves *you.*

Did you notice that this reminder is *personal?*

God was in a covenant relationship with the people of Israel. Even though they turned their backs on God, he would not turn his back on them. He was keeping a watchful eye on them. Two times in this promise from the book of Jeremiah, God used the personal pronoun *I.* He wanted the people of Israel to know that he hadn't forgotten them. He was involved in what was going on.

It's the same with you. To God, you are not just one of the 7.8 billion people on the planet. You are his child; he's been part of and had a plan for your life since you were in the womb. For God, when it comes to you, it's personal.

And did you also notice that this reminder tells us that our personal God has *plans*?

Three times in one verse, God used the word *plans*. God had plans to both prosper Israel and give them hope and a future. God's plans never fail. They can never be thwarted. Sometimes it feels as though our mess has maybe messed up God's plans. But God can take our mistakes, our failures, and even our sins and work them as part of his design. Paul wrote to the church in Rome, "We know that in all things God works for the good of those who love him, who have been called according to his purpose" (Romans 8:28).

I have an aunt who used to cross-stitch. As a kid, I would stay at her house from time to time during the summer. I would watch her sew the thread through a specific pattern. When she took a break, I would look at the cross-stitch in process and have no idea what she was creating. Even after she was done, if you flipped the fabric to its backside, there was no way you could make out the picture or writing.

This reminds me of God's plans. Often we are looking at the backside of the cross-stitch he is sewing. From our perspective, all we see are random strands of cut-up, unconnected thread that don't seem to go together or make any sense. But from his perspective, God sees a beautiful tapestry that he is knitting together. It's *not* random pieces of thread; God is weaving together a rope called hope.

THE POWER OF A PAUSE

I bet Bartimaeus didn't think God had a plan for him. The Bible tells us that he was a blind beggar (Mark 10:46). It's hard to imagine a worse spot to be in. Talk about hopeless.

Think what it would be like to never see the beauty of God's creation: a sunrise or sunset, a sky full of stars, or the vastness of the ocean.

Imagine being totally dependent on others, needing help with the basic necessities of life, like eating, getting dressed, and using the restroom.

This was Bartimaeus. His blindness led to his poverty. He couldn't see, and therefore he couldn't work. In those times, Bartimaeus would have been at just about the lowest rung of the social ladder. People might have despised a tax collector more, but at least a tax collector had resources. Bartimaeus had nothing. We could simply write one word across his life: *hopeless.*

One day Bartimaeus heard that Jesus was walking through the city of Jericho on his way to Jerusalem. This was near the very end of Jesus's ministry, and the Bible says a "large crowd" (verse 46) was surrounding him. Jesus had recently raised Lazarus from the dead, and I'm sure that news traveled fast.

We don't know how Bartimaeus knew about Jesus, but something he had heard gave him hope. He was not going to let Jesus pass him by. "When he heard that it was Jesus of Nazareth, he began to shout" (verse 47).

The word *shout* in the original language of the Bible indicates a guttural scream. It's the same word Mark used to describe a man filled with demons who screamed "with a shriek" (5:7, NLT). John used the word in Revelation to describe a woman "screaming in labor" (12:2, NET).[4] I was in the room when each of my four children was born. *Shouting* is a rather good description. And this is what Bartimaeus shouted: "Jesus, Son of David, have mercy on me!" (Mark 10:47).

Interesting, isn't it? Bartimaeus heard that "Jesus of Nazareth" was passing by. But that's not what he cried out. He screamed, "Jesus, Son of David, have mercy on me!"

Son of David is a messianic term used to describe the one who would sit on David's throne and govern Israel with all power and authority. In using that phrase, Bartimaeus was expressing his faith.

We don't know how he put two and two together, but something clicked. Maybe he had heard the promise Isaiah gave of a time when the Messiah would come and the deaf would hear, the blind would see, and the poor would rejoice (Isaiah 29:18–19). Perhaps his mom or dad had taught him those promises or a friend had told him those prophecies were being fulfilled by the miracle-working rabbi from Nazareth.

We don't know how Bartimaeus put it all together, but we do know that on this one afternoon, a blind man was seeing more clearly than anyone else in the crowd.

His screaming must have been loud and persistent, because evidently it was getting on people's nerves. Mark's gospel tells us, "Many rebuked him and told him to be quiet, but he shouted all the more, 'Son of David, have mercy on me!'" (10:48).

There are two reasons the crowd could not keep Bartimaeus from Jesus.

The first reason was Bartimaeus. The people rebuked him, but he cried out "all the more." This was his one shot at a new life. He had one hope, and that hope was about to walk by. He was going to get the attention of Jesus, and he was not going to be denied. His cry was loud. It was persistent. It was insistent. There was no way the crowd could stop him.

The second reason the crowd could not keep Bartimaeus from Jesus was Jesus. This entire passage in Mark's gospel hinges on two words: "Jesus stopped" (verse 49).

Wow. The power of a pause. Jesus was about to meet a need and change a life, and Bartimaeus was about to have hope—all because "Jesus stopped."

Jesus stopped what he was doing; he pushed pause on everything else going on, everything else he had to do. Why? For one man in need.

When I read this passage, it baffles me that the cry of this man stopped deity in his tracks. I've wondered how Jesus heard Bartimaeus's scream in the midst of what must have been a noisy crowd. How did he hear Bartimaeus?

I liken it to my wife when our kids were little. Debbie and I would be watching a movie in our living room. I would be completely into the movie. All of a sudden, Debbie would tell me to mute the TV. I would be so annoyed. *Why mute now? What's the issue? We're stopping right in the middle of the best part!*

She would simply say, "Listen." But I didn't hear anything. Then, just like clockwork, I would hear the noise she had already heard. From way upstairs, I would hear a baby crying or young children laughing when they were supposed to be sleeping. I swear that I never heard it when we were watching TV! But a mother's ears are *always* tuned to the cries of her children.

God's ears are also always tuned to the cries of his children. Jesus's ears were tuned to the cry of Bartimaeus. Jesus stopped and then called him. Bartimaeus must have felt as though he'd just won the lottery. (You know, the Jericho lottery they all played back then.) It was like winning on *The Price Is Right*. Jesus was telling Bartimaeus to "come on down!" Bartimaeus ran over.

> "What do you want me to do for you?" Jesus asked him.
>
> The blind man said, "Rabbi, I want to see."
>
> "Go," said Jesus, "your faith has healed you." Immediately he received his sight and followed Jesus along the road. (verses 51–52)

Hope fulfilled after one cry.
Hope fulfilled after one request.

Hope fulfilled after one exchange with Jesus.

If you need an infusion of hope, that should do it.

NOT OUR HOME

Dick and Marvel have had to bury both of their kids. I can't imagine having to do that.

In writing this chapter, I asked them some questions. I asked, "Have you ever felt like you were losing hope?" Dick admitted that there have been moments. As a dad, he saw it as his responsibility to fix things, but he couldn't fix Kurt's accident or Amy's cancer.

Marvel answered with a short statement that elementary kids could remember and repeat. Years of teaching kindergarten made her a master communicator. She said, "This is not our home."

How do they keep going? They hold on to hope and the truth of God's Word. Dick's life verse is this:

We do not lose heart. Though outwardly we are wasting away, yet inwardly we are being renewed day by day. For our light and momentary troubles are achieving for us an eternal glory that far outweighs them all. So we fix our eyes not on what is seen, but on what is unseen, since what is seen is temporary, but what is unseen is eternal. (2 Corinthians 4:16–18)

Dick and Marvel have a different kind of hope, a better hope, because they are looking forward to a different kind of home, a better home. Someday they will spend the rest of their days there with Kurt and Amy. Dick told me that he gets tears in his eyes just imagining how good it will be to see them again. They will be in heaven—for *always*—because of Jesus.

Throughout the Bible, there are repeated mentions of scarlet thread or yarn. Red ropes find their way into a variety of Bible stories. Theologians have run with that idea and have spoken of the "scarlet thread through the Bible."[5] Jesus is that scarlet thread. It's like he is a rope running through and connecting all the Bible. And the blood that Jesus shed for us, his sacrifice that allows us to be with God now and forever, is what makes that rope red.

Hope has a rope. Hope also has a name. *Jesus* is that rope.

He is called our "blessed hope" (Titus 2:13) in Scripture, and he promises that one day he will return and make all things right. Believing this, we can have confidence in the blessed hope and know with certainty that the always God is *always here, always working,* and *always faithful.*

QUESTIONS FOR REFLECTION

~~~~~~~

Chapter 1: Always Seeing

1. Read Psalm 121. What does this psalm teach about God, and why should it give us confidence as believers?

2. Jarrett described God as being like a coach calling a game from a press box. God has a different perspective than we do. Is this helpful to think about as you process whether or not God sees what you are going through? Why or why not?

3. Do you ever feel like Hagar—that no one sees you or understands you? In what ways does God's name El Roi ("the God who sees") comfort and help you during those moments?

4. How can you share with struggling loved ones the comforting truth that God sees them?

5. Why should we begin with the fact that God always sees? How is this truth life changing for you and for others?

Chapter 2: Always Hearing

1. Do you ever feel as though your prayers don't make it past the ceiling? What truth can you lean on when that happens?

2. How can you know that God is actually listening to your prayers?

3. What are the two or three greatest invitations you've ever received? How should the invitation for conversation with God affect the way we pray?

4. What could possibly be causing your calls (prayers to God) to get blocked? Is there something in your life that you are cherishing more than you cherish God?

5. Jarrett wrote about a posture of humility when we pray. What are some ways you can foster humility in your life?

Chapter 3: Always Speaking

1. How do you typically respond when you feel like you cannot hear from God? How should you respond during those times?

2. Can you think of a moment when, looking back, you are certain that God was speaking to you? What did he say? If not, after reading this chapter, how can you better seek to hear his voice?

3. In this chapter, we read that God speaks to us through multiple ways: creation, conscience, circumstances, prayer and the Bible, the Holy Spirit, and wise counsel. In which of these ways do you regularly experience God speaking to you? In which of these ways do you rarely experience God speaking to you?

4. How would you respond if someone were to ask, "Do you really hear God speak to you?" What would you say?

5. How does God speak to us in the silence? Why is silence so hard to achieve today, and how can you take steps to create daily times of silence and hearing from God?

Chapter 4: Pursuing the Lost

1. Do you remember a time in your life when you were lost? What was that like?

2. How does God actively pursue the lost?

3. Do you pursue the lost in your life? Discuss with your small group one person whom you believe God is pursuing through your intentional efforts and prayers.

4. What was Jarrett referring to when he described the Hound of heaven? What does that mean for you and the lost people in your life?
5. When the lost come home, what is the appropriate response?
6. How does the story of Jarrett's brother affect you and the way you pray for or minister to the lost?

Chapter 5: Restoring the Broken

1. We love stories of restoration (whether we love *Fixer Upper* or not!). Why is restoration so powerful?
2. Read the poem "The Touch of the Master's Hand" from this chapter again. How does God's hand in our lives fix what is broken and make us valuable?
3. In what ways have our hearts become hard like dry Play-Doh? What should we do when our hearts are becoming hard to God?
4. The Gospels are full of stories in which Jesus redeems broken sinners. In this chapter, we read about the woman caught in adultery and Peter. What is another story of Jesus redeeming someone who was broken? How has he redeemed you?
5. Jeff and Cheryl have been powerfully redeemed by God and now use their redemption story to help others. How can you use your story to minister to and help others who are broken and struggling? Can you name one person you can reach out to today to encourage?

Chapter 6: Calming the Anxious

1. Have you ever struggled with anxiety? Are you close to anyone who struggles with it? If so, what causes you or your loved one the most anxiety?
2. How has the Lord offered you comfort when you were scared or stressed?

3. Do you ever feel like the disciples in the storm when they asked Jesus if he cared? Why is it hard for us to remember that Jesus can control the storm?

4. What are the exercises Jarrett writes about for calming anxiety? Which are easiest for you, and which are most difficult?

5. Talk through this statement: "What is over your head is under His feet." Do you believe this? Why or why not?

Chapter 7: Encouraging the Fearful

1. How does this chapter change your perspective on how you should respond to fear? Why should you face your fears instead of fleeing from them?

2. Think back to the men and women of the Bible who faced their fears. How did they do so, and what does this teach you about facing your own fears?

3. Have you ever thought about fear and Christmas? What role does fear have in the Christmas story?

4. God is with us. God is for us. God is in us. Which of these three truths is most powerful and helpful to you personally? Which of these three truths do you struggle with the most?

5. In your small group, name one fear that overwhelms you. Take time to pray with someone else in your small group, asking God to fill you with faith to face your deepest fear.

Chapter 8: Comforting the Lonely

1. Describe a time when you have felt lonely.

2. How does the fact that we are made in the image of God affect the way we view loneliness?

3. What is the difference between being alone and being lonely?

4. How can God's faithfulness in the past comfort you today?

5. Do you know people who struggle with loneliness? If you

could share one Scripture verse or Bible story to encourage them, what would it be?

Chapter 9: Helping the Angry

1. Do you view anger as a big deal? Are you surprised that Jesus equates anger to murder in the Sermon on the Mount (Matthew 5)? In that passage, what is Jesus saying about anger and the attitude we should have toward it?

2. If anger comes out of the heart, how do we follow Solomon's instructions to guard our hearts and protect them from the dangers of anger?

3. In this chapter, we read that we have several choices for dealing with our anger: repress it, rehearse it, release it, or replace it. What do you usually choose to do with your anger? How can you better replace it with God's forgiveness?

4. What did you learn from the example of how Jesus forgave others? How can you apply Jesus's example to your own life?

5. Are you dealing with anger right now? Is there someone you need to forgive? Talk with your small-group members about it, and ask them to pray for you.

Chapter 10: Forgiving the Guilty

1. What is something that you feel guilty about?

2. Look back at the guilt paradigm. What is the difference between conviction and condemnation?

3. Read Romans 8:1. What does this verse teach about living free from condemnation?

4. List the three choices we make every day to walk in freedom. Which is the hardest of the three choices for you to make?

5. Why is confession so important in relation to forgiveness?

Chapter 11: Trust in God

1. How does remembering God's past faithfulness help us to better trust him with our present faithfulness? Think about and write down a few times when God has been faithful to you this past year.

2. God is our father and our shepherd. How do these images of him help you to better trust him in the big and small areas of life?

3. Why are coffee-cup Bible verses so powerful? How have you seen these Bible verses used in good ways, and how have you seen them used the wrong way?

4. How does the question "What's it going to take more faith to do?" shape how you will make your next big decision? What role does faith make in our decision-making processes?

5. What would you say to someone who is having a hard time trusting God? What has been helpful for you when you are struggling to trust God?

Chapter 12: Hope in God

1. Has there ever been a time when a situation you faced seemed hopeless? If yes, describe that time.

2. What does it mean that God has plans for you? How is this hopeful to you?

3. Repeat this out loud: "God loves me and is for me." Is this hard for you to believe? Why or why not?

4. How did hope motivate Bartimaeus? How should it motivate you?

5. "Hope has a rope. Hope also has a name. *Jesus* is that rope." Do you know Jesus? Write down three reasons why with Jesus there is always hope.

ACKNOWLEDGMENTS

~~~~~~

The writing process is a journey. I am thankful for the encouragement and support of so many people along the way who have helped make this project a reality.

To my wife, Debbie. No one sacrifices more than you. Thank you for believing in me and pushing me to fulfill God's calling on my life. You make Team Stephens go. I love you.

To our girls, Riley, Kelsey, Landry, and Cameron. It is the joy of my life to be your dad. I hope you will carry the message of this book with you forever. I'll tell you this as long as I have breath: "God has great plans for your life. Always keep your mind, heart, and eyes on him."

This book was edited during my transition from being the teaching pastor at Prestonwood Baptist Church in Plano, Texas, to becoming the senior pastor at Champion Forest Baptist Church in Houston, Texas. It was an honor to serve the Prestonwood faith family for over twenty years. I am eternally grateful for your support and encouragement. Thank you for loving me and my family so well. Thank you, Dr. Jack Graham, for your friendship to me and your influence in my life.

To Champion Forest Baptist Church. Thank you for calling me to serve as your senior pastor. I count it a privilege to come to "work" every day and partner with a staff team that is second to none. I am so excited about the future God has for us as we seek to reach as many people as possible with the good news of Jesus. Let's keep working together to advance the kingdom in northwest Houston and beyond.

Everyone needs friends in ministry who believe the best of you, build you up, and hold you accountable. Jeff Young, Connor Bales, Michael Neale, Chris Kouba, Brad Lewter, and Nick Floyd. Thank you for being such incredible friends to me. I am a better man because of each of you.

To Shannon Dick, Jack Raymond, and J. D. Lowrie. Thank you for poring over this manuscript and offering valuable feedback. Also, thank you for assisting me with research and specifically for helping write the study questions offered in this book. I believe your efforts will enable and inspire a lot of people to grow in their faith.

To Don Gates. Thank you for allowing me to be part of the Gates Group. None of this happens without you. I am so grateful for how you have championed me and these past two book projects. Your wisdom, counsel, and friendship mean more than you know. Also, thank you for introducing me to Vince Antonucci. Vince, you made this book better. Thank you for coaching me and helping me throughout the writing process. I hope this is the first of many projects we collaborate on together.

Finally, to the whole team at WaterBrook Multnomah, including Abby DeBenedittis and Douglas Mann. Thank you for your creativity, insight, and expertise. A very special thanks is due to Paul Pastor. You have been a great advocate for me and personally engaged in this book from start to finish. I am thankful for how you have treated this project as your own.

NOTES

Chapter 1: Always Seeing

1. *Monsters, Inc.*, directed by Pete Doctor, David Silverman, and Lee Unkrich (Emeryville, CA: Pixar Animation Studios, 2001).
2. Garth Brooks, "Unanswered Prayers," *No Fences*, Capital Nashville, 1990.
3. Talia Avakian, "Here's How Many Planes Are in the Air at Any Moment," *Travel + Leisure*, May 19, 2017, www.travelandleisure.com/airlines-airports/number-of-planes-in-air.
4. John Piper, "God Is Always Doing 10,000 Things in Your Life," Desiring God, January 1, 2013, www.desiringgod.org/articles/god-is-always-doing-10000-things-in-your-life.

Chapter 2: Always Hearing

1. Lexico.com, s.v. "cherish," Oxford University Press, 2020, www.lexico.com/en/definition/cherish.
2. J. Vernon McGee, "James Study Guide," Thru the Bible, https://ttb.org/resources/study-guides/james-study-guide; Eusebius, *The Ecclesiastical History of Eusebius Pamphilus*, trans. Christian Frederick Crusé (Philadelphia: J. B. Lippincott, 1860), 76, www.google.com/books/edition/The_Ecclesiastical_History_of_Eusebius_P/dClHAQAAMAAJ.
3. "Tim Tebow Biography," Biography.com, updated January 20, 2020, www.biography.com/athlete/tim-tebow.
4. Michael Klopman, "Tebowing 101: Everything You Need to Know Behind Tim Tebow Phenomenon," *Huffington Post*, updated January 3, 2012, www.huffpost.com/entry/tebowing-101-tim-tebow-jared-kleinstein_n_1072374.
5. Mark Batterson, *The Circle Maker: Praying Circles Around Your Biggest Dreams and Greatest Fears* (Grand Rapids, MI: Zondervan, 2011), 152.
6. For example, Deuteronomy 9:25–26 (prostrate); 2 Samuel 7:18 (sitting); 2 Kings 4:35 (pacing); 2 Chronicles 6:12–14 (hands lifted); 2 Chronicles 20:5–6 (standing).

Chapter 3: Always Speaking

1. Polly House, "'Experiencing God' Is Subject of LifeWay Films Documentary," LifeWay Newsroom, April 30, 2013, https://blog.lifeway.com/newsroom/2013/04/30/experiencing-god-is-subject-of-lifeway-films-documentary.

2. Henry T. Blackaby and Claude V. King, *Experiencing God: Knowing and Doing the Will of God*, 15th anniversary ed. (Nashville: Broadman, Holman, 2004), 137.

3. Blackaby and King, *Experiencing God*, 133.

4. Blackaby and King, *Experiencing God*, 134.

5. Blackaby and King, *Experiencing God*, 134.

6. Blackaby and King, *Experiencing God*, 134.

7. Rebecca Barlow Jordan, "Eight Ways God Speaks to Us Today," Rebecca Barlow Jordan, 2017, www.rebeccabarlowjordan.com/eight-ways-god-speaks-to-us-today.

8. C. S. Lewis, *The Problem of Pain*, in *The Complete C. S. Lewis Signature Classics* (San Francisco: HarperSanFrancisco, 1996/2002), 406.

9. Oswald Chambers, "June 15: Get a Move On," in *My Utmost for His Highest*, classic ed. (Grand Rapids, MI: Discovery House, 2017).

Chapter 4: Pursuing the Lost

1. Cara Morgan, "Lost and Found: The Average American Spends 2.5 Days Each Year Looking for Lost Items Collectively Costing U.S. Households $2.7 Billion Annually in Replacement Costs," PR Newswire, May 2, 2017, www.prnewswire.com/news-releases/lost-and-found-the-average-american-spends-25-days-each-year-looking-for-lost-items-collectively-costing-us-households-27-billion-annually-in-replacement-costs-300449305.html.

2. "660. Apollymi," New Testament Lexical Aids in *Hebrew Greek Key Word Study Bible: New International Version* (AMG International, 1996), 1591.

3. "Lexicon: Strong's G622—apollymi," Blue Letter Bible, www.blueletterbible.org/lang/lexicon/lexicon.cfm?Strongs=G622&t=KJV.

4. Everard Meynell, *The Life of Francis Thompson* (London: Burns and Oates, 1913), www.gutenberg.org/files/45106/45106-h/45106-h.htm.

5. John Thomson, *Francis Thompson: The Preston-Born Poet*, 2nd ed. (London: Simpkin, Marshall, Hamilton, Kent, and Co., 1913), 28–31, https://archive.org/details/francisthompsonpoothom/page/34/mode/2up.

6. Francis Thompson, *The Hound of Heaven* (New York: Dodd, Mead, 1922/1930), 45.

7. J. F. X. O'Conor, *A Study of Francis Thompson's Hound of Heaven*, 4th ed. (New York: John Lane Company, 1912), 7, https://archive.org/details/studyoffrancisthoooconrich/page/6/mode/2up.

8. Charles Spurgeon, "Many Kisses for Returning Sinners, or Prodigal Love for the Prodigal Son" (sermon no. 2236, Metropolitan Tabernacle, Newington, London, March 29, 1891), https://archive.spurgeon.org/sermons/2236.php.

9. Kool and the Gang, "Celebration," *Celebrate!*, Warner Chappell Music, 1981.

10. William Barclay, *The Gospel of Luke, The New Daily Study Bible* (Louisville, KY: Westminster John Knox, 1975/2001), 240.

11. Rob Russell (@roblrussell), "Packed house, so people have started sitting outside," Twitter, February 13, 2013, https://twitter.com/roblrussell/status/298103300757258240.

Chapter 5: Restoring the Broken

1. Mike Copeland, "Waco Tourist Attractions Have Another Banner Year Boosted by Magnolia," *Waco Tribune-Herald*, December 29, 2018, https://wacotrib.com/business/waco-tourist-attractions-have-another-banner-year-boosted-by-magnolia/article_043dd3b6-5773-5c97-bdab-1068f952a11e.html.

2. Myra Brooks Welch, "The Touch of the Master's Hand," All Poetry, https://allpoetry.com/The-Touch-of-the-Master's-Hand.

3. "8845. Šāḥaṭ," Old Testament Lexical Aids in *Hebrew Greek Key Word Study Bible: New International Version* (AMG International, 1996), 1557.

4. For instance, Romans 8:18–19; 2 Corinthians 3:18; Philippians 3:20–21; Colossians 3:4; 1 John 3:2.

Chapter 6: Calming the Anxious

1. "What Is Stress?," American Institute of Stress, www.stress.org/daily-life.

2. Keith Hampton et al., "Psychological Stress and Media Use," *Social Media and the Cost of Caring*, Pew Research, January 15, 2015, www.pewresearch.org/internet/2015/01/15/psychological-stress-and-social-media-use-2.

3. Stephanie Watson and Kristeen Cherney, "The Effects of Sleep Deprivation on Your Body," Healthline, May 15, 2020, www.healthline.com/health/sleep-deprivation/effects-on-body.

4. Strong's Concordance, s.v. "*megas*," Bible Hub, https://biblehub.com/greek/3173.htm.

5. "Seinfeld The Marine Biologist," YouTube video, 14:25, from episode 78 of. *Seinfeld*, televised February 10, 1994, posted by "EremiT," January 18, 2012, www.youtube.com/watch?v=Oy5m4m8GayQ.

6. HELPS Word-studies, s.v. "1510. *eimi*," Bible Hub, https://biblehub.com/greek/1510.htm.

7. "337. Anankazō," New Testament Lexical Aids in *Hebrew Greek Key Word Study Bible: New International Version* (AMG International, 1996), 1584.

8. Adrian Rogers, "He Has Overcome the World," Love Worth Finding, May 30, 2009, www.lightsource.com/ministry/love-worth-finding/devotionals/love-worth-finding/love-worth-finding-may-30-11604151.html.

9. "'Father of Aerobics' Kenneth Cooper, MD, MPH, to Receive Healthy Cup Award from Harvard School of Public Health," Harvard School of Public Health News, April 16, 2008, www.hsph.harvard.edu/news/press-releases/aerobics-kenneth-cooper-to-receive-harvard-healthy-cup-award.

10. Max Lucado, *Great Day Every Day: Navigating Life's Challenges with Promise and Purpose* (Nashville: Thomas Nelson, 2012), 49, 125.

11. David Jeremiah, "January 2: Trading Stress for a Song," *Discovering God: 365 Daily Devotions* (Carol Stream, IL: Tyndale, 2015), 3.

Chapter 7: Encouraging the Fearful

1. "Frank Oz: Yoda," *Star Wars: Episode I—The Phantom Menance,* directed by George Lucas, Lucasfilm, 1999, www.imdb.com/title/tt0120915/characters/nm0000568.

2. "Ancient Marriage," Bible History Online, www.bible-history.com/biblestudy/marriage.html.

3. "seinfeld-public-speaking," YouTube video, :27, excerpt from "I'm Telling You for the Last Time," Jerry Seinfeld, stand-up comedy routine, 1998, posted by "ExplainItStudios," January 26, 2014, www.youtube.com/watch?v=yQ6giVKp9ec.

Chapter 8: Comforting the Lonely

1. George Cooke, "Joy in My Heart," 1926, public domain.

2. Foreigner, "Waiting for a Girl Like You," 4, Atlantic Records, 1981.

3. Some of the following examples were used in a sermon series preached by Jack Graham and me, and were also published in Jack Graham's book, *Help! Facing Life's Challenges with Confidence and Hope.*

4. Whitesnake, "Here I Go Again," *Saints & Sinners,* Sony/ATV Music Publishing, 1982.

5. Megan Brenan, "U.S. Adults Report Less Worry, More Happiness," Gallup, May 18, 2020, https://news.gallup.com/poll/311135/adults-report-less-worry-happiness.aspx.

6. Gabrielle Denman, "All the Lonely People: The Epidemic of Loneliness and Its Consequences," Social Science Works, https://socialscienceworks.org/all-the-lonely-people-the-epidemic-of-loneliness-and-its-consequences.

7. "Loneliness and the Workplace," Cigna, 2020, www.cigna.com/static/www-cigna-com/docs/about-us/newsroom/studies-and-reports/combatting-loneliness/cigna-2020-loneliness-factsheet.pdf.

8. Leland Kim, "Loneliness Linked to Serious Health Problems and Death Among Elderly," University of California San Francisco, June 18, 2012, www.ucsf.edu/news/2012/06/98644/loneliness-linked-serious-health-problems-and-death-among-elderly.

9. Timothy Keller, "Adam was not lonely because he was imperfect," Facebook, September 9, 2013, www.facebook.com/timkellernyc/posts/621239534582603.

10. Richard J. Foster, *Celebration of Discipline: The Path to Spiritual Growth,* 20th anniversary ed. (New York: HarperCollins, 1998), 96.

11. Oliver Balch, "AI and Me: Friendship Chatbots Are on the Rise, but Is There

a Gendered Design Flaw?," *The Guardian,* May 7, 2020, www.theguardian
.com/careers/2020/may/07/ai-and-me-friendship-chatbots-are-on-the-rise
-but-is-there-a-gendered-design-flaw.

12. Replika company profile, LinkedIn, www.linkedin.com/company/replikaai.

Chapter 9: Helping the Angry

1. Elizabeth Chang, "Americans Are Living in a Big 'Anger Incubator.' Experts
Have Tips for Regulating Our Rage," *Washington Post,* June 30, 2020, www
.washingtonpost.com/lifestyle/wellness/anger-control-protests-masks
-coronavirus/2020/06/29/a1e882d0-b279-11ea-8758-bfd1d045525a_story
.html.

2. "Jon Gries: Uncle Rico," *Napoleon Dynamite,* directed by Jared Hess, Fox
Searchlight Pictures, 2004, www.imdb.com/title/tt0374900/characters/
nm0340973.

3. June Hunt, *Anger: Facing the Fire Within,* Thoughts and Emotions Series
(Dubuque, IA: Kendall Hunt, n.d.).

4. Lydia Martin, "What Your Anger Reveals About You," Thrive Global, November 7, 2018, https://thriveglobal.com/stories/what-your-anger-reveals
-about-you.

5. Hunt, *Anger,* 37.

Chapter 10: Forgiving the Guilty

1. *Merriam-Webster,* s.v. "guilt," www.merriam-webster.com/dictionary/guilt.

2. *Merriam-Webster,* s.v. "shame," www.merriam-webster.com/dictionary/
shame.

Chapter 11: Trust in God

1. "Peter Berg Reveals the Inspiration Behind 'Clear Eyes, Full Hearts, Can't
Lose,'" Yahoo! Sports, February 16, 2017, https://sports.yahoo.com/news/
peter-berg-reveals-the-inspiration-behind-clear-eyes-full-hearts-cant-lose
-215844638.html.

2. "The Charles Blondin Story," Creative Bible Study, www.creativebiblestudy
.com/Blondin-story.html.

3. Chris Tomlin, "Good Good Father," *Never Lose Sight,* sixstepsrecords, 2016.

4. "How Worrying Affects the Body," WebMD, September 12, 2020, www
.webmd.com/balance/guide/how-worrying-affects-your-body#1.

5. Debra J. Brody and Qiuping Gu, "Antidepressant Use Among Adults: United
States, 2015–2018," NCHS Data Brief no. 377, September 2020, www.cdc
.gov/nchs/products/databriefs/db377.htm.

6. "Major Depression," National Institute of Mental Health, February 2019,
www.nimh.nih.gov/health/statistics/major-depression.shtml.

7. Mandy Oaklander, "New Hope for Depression," *Time,* July 27, 2017, https://
time.com/4876098/new-hope-for-depression.

8. "Lexicon: Strong's H7725—*shwub*," Blue Letter Bible, www.blueletterbible .org/lang/lexicon/lexicon.cfm?Strongs=H7725&t=KJV.

9. Max Lucado, *Traveling Light: Releasing the Burdens You Were Never Intended to Bear* (Nashville: Thomas Nelson, 2001), 187–90.

10. "9128. Šā'an," Old Testament Lexical Aids in *Hebrew Greek Key Word Study Bible: New International Version* (AMG International, 1996), 1559.

11. *Brown-Driver-Briggs Hebrew and English Lexicon,* s.v. "yada," Bible Hub, 2006, https://biblehub.com/hebrew/3045.htm.

12. A. W. Tozer, *The Pursuit of God: The Definitive Classic,* ed. James L. Snyder (Ventura, CA: Regal, 2013), 22.

Chapter 12: Hope in God

1. Barry Popik, "You Can Live Three Weeks Without Food, Three Days Without Water, but Not a Moment Without Hope," Big Apple, April 27, 2013, www.barrypopik.com/index.php/new_york_city/entry/you_can_live_three_weeks_without_food_three_days_without_water_but_not_a_mo.

2. "Billy Graham, Evangelist to the World, Dead at Age 99," Billy Graham Evangelistic Association, February 21, 2018, https://billygraham.org/story/billy-graham-evangelist-to-the-world-dead-at-age-99.

3. Billy Graham, foreword to *Hope for the Troubled Heart: Finding God in the Midst of Pain (Nashville:* Thomas Nelson, 1991), ix.

4. Strong's Exhaustive Concordance, s.v. "2896. *krazō,*" Bible Hub, https://biblehub.com/greek/2896.htm.

5. W. A. Criswell, *The Scarlet Thread Through the Bible* (Nashville: LifeWay, 2014), www.gospelproject.com/wp-content/uploads/tgp2018/2018/04/The -Scarlet-Thread-Criswell.pdf.

ABOUT THE AUTHOR

~~~~~~

JARRETT STEPHENS serves as the senior pastor of Champion Forest Baptist Church in northwest Houston, one of the largest and most diverse churches in America. Pastor Jarrett previously served as the teaching pastor of Prestonwood Baptist Church, in Plano, Texas.

He began his ministry at Prestonwood as an intern, working with married adults in 2000, then grew into leadership in many roles, including overseeing the residency program, ministering to young singles, leading many mission trips, and launching the Prestonwood Network, which plants churches around the country.

Jarrett also serves on the boards of BridgeBuilders, Dallas Baptist University, and the North American Mission Board, which all point to his passions: sharing the life-transforming message of the gospel to the uttermost parts of the world, serving the least of these in the inner cities, raising up the next generation of Christian leaders, and equipping churches to be on mission.

A native of Louisiana, Jarrett graduated from Ouachita Baptist University in Arkadelphia, Arkansas, with a bachelor of arts in biblical studies and psychology. He received his master of divinity from Southwestern Baptist Theological Seminary in 2006 and his doctorate of ministry from Liberty Theological Seminary in 2012.

Jarrett is the author of two books. His debut book, *The Mountains Are Calling: Making the Climb for a Clearer View of God and Ourselves,* was released in 2018. In this book, Jarrett takes readers to ten mountaintop moments in the Bible where people had encounters with God. Through these experiences, God revealed his truth and brought his people closer to him.

Jarrett and his wife, Debbie, have four daughters: Riley, Kelsey, Cameron, and Landry.

Ascend the Mountaintop
Moments of the Bible

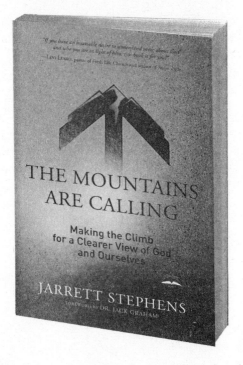

When God wanted to reveal a truth to his prophets and people,
it often involved a mountain because God loves taking us to places that
change our perspective of who he is—and who we are.

It is from these mountaintop moments that we then begin the real adventure—
reentering our world with a fresh perspective for making a difference.

MULTNOMAH